The New Economy Excellence Series

New Economy Expression:
Redefining Marketing in the Multichannel Age

David Mercer

JOHN WILEY & SONS, LTD

Chichester • New York • Weinheim • Brisbane • Singapore • Toronto

Copyright © 2001 by David Mercer

Published 2001 by John Wiley & Sons Ltd,
Baffins Lane, Chichester,
West Sussex PO19 1UD, England

National   01243 779777
International (+44) 1243 779777
e-mail (for orders and customer service enquiries):
    cs-books@wiley.co.uk
Visit our Home Page on http://www.wiley.co.uk
              or http://www.wiley.com

Other Wiley Editorial Offices

John Wiley & Sons, Inc., 605 Third Avenue,
New York, NY 10158-0012, USA

WILEY-VCH Verlag GmbH, Pappelallee 3,
D-69469 Weinheim, Germany

John Wiley & Sons, Australia Ltd, 33 Park Road, Milton,
Queensland 4064, Australia

John Wiley & Sons (Asia) Pte Ltd, 2 Clementi Loop #02-01,
Jin Xing Distripark, Singapore 129809

John Wiley & Sons (Canada) Ltd, 22 Worcester Road,
Rexdale, Ontario M9W 1L1, Canada

British Library Cataloguing in Publication Data

A catalogue record for this book is available from the British Library

ISBN 0-471-50008-9

Typeset in 11/14pt Garamond by Mayhew Typesetting, Rhayader, Powys
Printed and bound in Great Britain by Antony Rowe Ltd, Chippenham, Wiltshire
This book is printed on acid-free paper responsibly manufactured from
sustainable forestry, in which at least two trees are planted for each
one used for paper production.

CONTENTS

E$^+$synergy

CHAPTER 1

Overview

This is a book which deliberately approaches the much over-hyped new topic, e-commerce, from the pragmatic viewpoint of a traditional organisation which is now extending its existing operations into this field. This is because, for the foreseeable future, the most productive growth will take place in this area.

An introduction to E$^+$marketing

Over the next decade e-commerce, and the e-marketing which drives it, will have a dramatic impact on business across the board. That much is already evident. Yet much of that marketing will be based on the *traditional* marketing approaches with which we are so familiar, and which have worked so well for the past half century. The fascination, and certainly the media hype, may well come from the life and death dramas of the new dot.com start-ups, but these will be peripheral to the really important developments. Instead, as this book shows, the key activities will be those which allow existing, conventional businesses to *extend* their marketing operations into the field of e-commerce – and then to productively *integrate* the resulting developments into their mainstream strategies and operations. To highlight this difference, I refer to this more productive approach to the overall e-commerce environment as **e$^+$marketing**.

This book, therefore, takes as its starting point the likelihood that – based on your experience to date in traditional markets – you already appreciate how much of e-marketing works, since it is very much the same as that which you

> **KEY CONCEPT**
>
> E⁺marketing uses the extension into e-commerce to build an integrated approach, powerfully combining the best of the old and new.

have already practised. The role of the book, in this context, is to show you how this basic marketing theory needs to change in the e-commerce environment – and how it may then be best applied. Such incremental change, which at the same time balances the new requirements of e-commerce with the ongoing needs of the conventional business, is the key to **effective e⁺marketing**.

As a secondary objective, the book also sets out to act as an antidote to the hype, in that it focuses on the incremental growth of e-commerce as experienced by existing businesses – the 'clicks

> **KEY CONCEPT**
>
> Effective e⁺marketing builds on your existing marketing knowledge and skills.

and mortar' operators – which are rarely featured in the news but which, rather than the short-lived start-ups, already make up the most substantial part of the e-commerce boom.

Genuine one-to-one customer relationship management

The more important aspects of this 'revolution' come from our new-found abilities to mass market one-to-one. The new electronic media enable us to communicate on a truly personal basis – interacting with our customers as individuals – across the world!

> **KEY CONCEPT**
>
> E⁺marketing can become the optimum form of Customer Relationship Marketing (CRM)

Before e-commerce started to emerge, but after it had become so

obvious that *relationship marketing* was becoming the key to long-term success, we formulated a short (but comprehensive) new definition of marketing as:

> Marketing is both a *relationship* with the customer, based upon a series of transactions which, over time, should result in mutual benefit, and a parallel *dialogue* between you and the customer(s), which communicates the information necessary to define the 'relationship'.

It is now easy to see that this has become even more applicable to e-commerce, with its fundamental emphasis on interaction! Indeed, that interactive element, rather than any new information communications technology (ICT), is what differentiates those aspects of marketing which are changed by the new medium.

On the other hand, it is important to note that these changes – although they are very important in general and quite central in specific sectors – are *incremental*. This book will stress that the most important parts of marketing are those you have *already* learned in the context of traditional markets. We will, therefore, build upon your existing knowledge to see how the new elements may be productively incorporated into your existing business practices.

I once had the unhappy experience of attending a three-day workshop taught by one of the leading sales training organisations. We spent three days learning about their techniques (perhaps better described as gimmicks), which revolved around 'persuading' the poor victim to place an order he or she didn't want (perhaps not the ideal approach, where trust is so important for long-term relationships). The climax, however, was an exhortation: 'Forget all your previous experience and just use the ideas we have taught you in these three days.' In view of the gimmicky nature of the material, it would have been poor advice even for a new salesperson, but

– as I looked around the ten or so senior sales executives gathered there – I worked out that the advice could have been rephrased as, 'Throw away a hundred man years of successful experience!' Much of what is now being taught about 'e-commerce marketing' seems, to me at least, to adopt the same cavalier approach to the experience we have over decades painstakingly built up in marketing. This book definitely does not throw that very lusty baby out with the bath-water! It quite deliberately *builds* upon existing experience to create a very productive *synergy* between the old and new.

As a result of the e⁺marketing approach, *building on existing marketing skills*, the approach of this book is much closer to the straightforward approach adopted by some of the better (traditional) marketing texts than to the more trendy new books about start-ups.

Thus, this book starts with the customer, and in particular with (one-to-one) relationship management, before reviewing the impact of e-commerce on the more traditional elements of the marketing mix. It then looks at the new services demanded by such e-commerce, using the well understood models of e-tail and in particular direct marketing as an introduction to these, before examining some of the more specific developments, such as advertising. After a short review of business-to-business (B2B) e-commerce, which is often more about integrating operations management systems than communicating over the Internet, it ends by looking at some predictions for the medium- and longer-term – especially in terms of the home-based customer-to-customer (C2C) markets which will eventually become the most valuable of all.

KEY CONCEPT

To provide further help, the key concepts are also highlighted as marginal notes throughout the book.

This book is full of ideas you can use in your own work, including many action checklists. To help you assess your needs we suggest that you note your answers to these questions (usually denoted by ■) as you go along.

However, there is no escaping a brief introduction to the technology. As an enabler, at least, this can be central to developments, so I can't avoid it; though, if you are already well versed in the subject, you can skip to the third chapter! But I can, and will, keep it as short and painless as possible!

Controlled anarchy: the background to e-commerce

CHAPTER 2

OVERVIEW

Some appreciation of the technology underpinning
e-commerce, and its various categories, is needed to
provide the context for the rest of the book. This brief
chapter, therefore, aims at giving you the bare minimum
of technical knowledge you will need. As I have already
suggested, if you already feel comfortable with this
technology you can skip this chapter, and get to grips
with Customer Relationship Management (CRM), in
Chapter 3, which lies at the heart of the most important
developments.

- Information Communications Technology (ICT) as
  an enabler
- Stages in developing an e-commerce business
- Incremental additions needed for e-commerce
- Definitions of e-commerce
- E-commerce categories, especially B2C and B2B

Information communications technology (ICT)

The importance of e-commerce is encapsulated in e-marketing, not in the IT technology that makes it possible, so I will only briefly recapitulate this aspect.

> **KEY CONCEPT**
>
> Successful e-commerce comes from effective marketing, not ICT.

To start to put this book into context, I will quote a senior manager from a leading multinational, who succinctly pointed out that '. . . the performance of ICT in general will get a million or more times better in the not too distant future.' What this means is that we already have the capability of doing almost anything we might ever want to do with computers. That capability is already built into the personal computers we now have on our office desks. Soon it will be scattered around the home, built into every electronic gadget, even our toasters!

Equally, the communications aspects of the revolution will prove to have an ever-greater impact. Already there is virtually no cost involved in setting up a data link to the other side of the world, even for video. The fact that telephone companies still charge large sums of money for this is only because they have, for the time being, a monopoly which enables them to do this. That monopoly will soon disappear. So work will become distance-independent – which will have a significant impact on the e-commerce revolution and indeed on society as a whole.

Even from the point of view of technology, the details of this will, however, be largely irrelevant. Forget how fast your chip will run. The only significant practical difference in the near future will be that data entry will

> **KEY CONCEPT**
>
> The ICT technology can already do anything we might want.

become much easier. For example, I am dictating this book into my handheld dictating machine. This then plugs into my

PC and my spoken words are converted into the printed form you see. Today, this is relatively unusual but, with a number of firms in Silicon Valley racing to produce mass-market versions, it will soon become the norm. We will no longer have to spend hours typing at our keyboards. More importantly, a wider group of users – those who are frightened by keyboards – will be able to join the 'computer literate'.

Even so, most people still think of the hardware as making up the ICT revolution, but – as I have said – all you need to know is that very soon it really will enable us to do everything we might ever want. The skill is in deciding exactly what you *do* want! In fact, it is the new software that will enable us to do much more. In particular, it should improve once the Microsoft (see http://microsoft.com) monopoly is broken, albeit by its competitors rather than the US Department of Justice! People in the industry reckon that Microsoft's stranglehold, forcing us into one particular standard – the Windows standard, which has been less than ideal for global Internet communications – has held us back by something like ten years! It has made Bill Gates a very rich man but it has impoverished the rest of us.

The Internet

In this chapter, I don't intend to spend much time on Internet 'technology'. Again, you will probably already have read everything you might ever need to know about it – even if much of the material is likely to have been hype rather than fact. Just one point about its history though, because it indicates some of the special strengths and weaknesses of the Internet. Many people, from a US Vice-President down, have claimed to have started it, but its origins were, in fact, within the US Department of Defence – with a system called ARPAnet which was designed to survive nuclear attack!

Accordingly, the key element that ARPAnet brought into our modern world was the idea that all the bits and pieces had to operate by themselves. This resulted in a form of anarchy, and means that – in essence – the Internet is still anarchic. It is uncontrollable. It can't be controlled by monopolies or by governments, or by anyone else – even by Bill Gates – which is a great virtue in an age where the multinationals can control almost everything else. Almost alone amongst 'commercial' bodies, it is a great democratic institution.

However, one of the most important remaining techno-logical developments will be that, in effect, the computer itself will *disappear*. It will become part of the fabric of our houses and offices around us. It will consist of a hidden network of many different components, all round the house, connected by radio. As you wander round the rooms you will be able to tell it exactly what to do, as you might any servant. In fact the new (Bluetooth) radio technology will mean that you won't need any other communications systems.

One important point to note, however, is that – at least in terms of the communications aspects – the model for much of this will no longer be the office computer. It will be the telephone, which we have used for the best part of a century, but it will be cheaper and easier to use than the telephone. Desktop computers are really a clumsy amalgam of a television set (to see the data) and a keyboard (to enter it). Before the Internet, it was most often used as a combination of typewriter and calculator. However, it is now being used to broaden our horizons, to give us access to a whole world of information. That represents a change in the future of humanity.

Before we leave the subject of technology, or at least the world of the technophiles, it is worth pointing out that their view of the world is centred on the technology. Hence, e-business, as they would describe it, makes almost no reference to the normal world as we recognise it. The reality is, as we will see later, that the technology is merely an *enabler*. It is what we, and society, decide that is important.

On the other hand, far too few companies take any notice of the Internet. At the beginning of the new millennium, a Reuters survey[1] of the Fortune 100 in the US showed that 40% of companies had failed to take the Internet seriously, with around a quarter of them not even being contactable by email!

Claims that Internet technology will dramatically reduce costs have rarely been born out in experience. Indeed *The Economist*[2] suggests that it is only 'errand jobs' that have been displaced by the Internet or by ICT in general. On the other hand, even removing 'errand jobs' does contribute significantly – by taking away a lot of the minor irritations which otherwise plague managers.

To summarise, despite the claims of the technophiles, the main lesson of ICT is that it should be seen as an *enabler*. In the near future the agenda may be set by ICT corporations, especially by Microsoft, but ulti-

> **KEY CONCEPT**
>
> ICT is only an enabler, what matters is what you choose to do with it.

mately it will be set by what *we* choose to do with it. As I have said earlier, the power to do whatever we want is already there to enable whatever we want. *It is now about making choices.*

A definition of e-commerce

Most textbooks start with a definition of the subject they are attempting to describe. Unfortunately, in trying to define e-commerce, we find that there are a significant number of possible definitions which sometimes overlap and even contradict each other, leading to confusion. At the most

---

[1] Reported by Reuters, London, 14 July 2000.
[2] *The Economist*, E-commerce: Too few pennies from heaven, 1 July 2000.

basic level some people suggest quite simply that it *covers everything about buying and selling products and services over the network*. They also emphasise that these transactions are over *electronic links* and that the commodity usually being traded is *information*. But, even though this is probably the most widely accepted version, it is still too general to be useful.

There are so many different definitions at a more detailed level that it sometimes seems as if you can create a new world simply by putting an 'e' in front of any existing business function. Not least, there is confusion between e-business –

> **KEY CONCEPT**
>
> e-Commerce potentially covers everything we might buy and sell, but does this electronically.

which perhaps covers everything done in an e-commerce company – and e-commerce itself – which may be the trading, marketing, part. In this book I will avoid these problems with semantics by referring to any business conducted through electronic trading links as 'e-commerce'; and I will not use a capital letter anywhere, for e-commerce is a business function like any other! You will note that even **e⁺marketing** uses a lower-case 'e'! Beyond that, the existing marketing vocabulary should be quite sufficient.

 GETTING STARTED: Growing into e-commerce

Perhaps more helpfully, some other people look at e-commerce not in terms of a definition but in terms of the *progress* companies make as they go ever more deeply into e-commerce. Typically this 'progress' consists of six different steps:

> **KEY CONCEPT**
>
> Organisations go through progressive stages of e-commerce development, from simple communication to sophisticated transformation.

- *Communication.* At this first stage the company typically sets up a website so that it can show the outside world that it has taken notice of the Internet – and, to a certain extent, it is willing to talk with that world through this new medium.

  Is this the stage your organisation is at?

- *Structured website.* At this stage the company begins to take the Internet seriously and starts to use its website to communicate effectively with the outside world. In particular, it structures itself so that the information on its website is in a useful form.

  Is this the stage your organisation is at?

- *Trying e-commerce.* This is where the organisation begins to see that the web, or at least the Internet, is a channel for doing business much like other parts of its distribution operation.

  Is this the stage your organisation is at?

- *Doing e-commerce.* Then it begins to take e-commerce seriously and links it to the legacy systems on its own computers and thence to the outside world through the Internet.

  Is this the stage your organisation is at?

- *Pervasive e-commerce.* This stage, which very few organisa-tions have yet reached, represents the complete integration of a company's e-commerce operations with the rest of its operations.

  Is this the stage your organisation is at?

- *Transformation.* Finally comes what some people call 'one world one computer', where barriers between the organisation and other organisations break down and they start to share one database which recognises no limits.

Is this the stage your organisation is at?

A practical view

In general, however, such definitions tend to focus rather too closely on the technology. As we already said, this really is just an enabler. Accordingly, I think one of the most useful approaches is that taken by Bernadette Tiernan,[3] who provides a number of useful recommendations, especially in terms of the incremental additions to existing business which are the focus of this book.

 Vital questions and answers

Take a long-range view
■ Does this apply to your organisation?

Sell products that are easy to identify
■ Does this apply to your organisation?

Capitalise on the value of product extensions
■ Does this apply to your organisation?

Provide services that are understandable
■ Does this apply to your organisation?

Recognise the potential in niche markets
■ Does this apply to your organisation?

Acquire prominent listings in the big portals
■ Does this apply to your organisation?

Install high-profile systems
■ Does this apply to your organisation?

---

[3] Tiernan, B. (2000) *E-Tailing*, Chicago, Dearborn.

The first four are, I think, the most useful:

- *Take a long-range view.*
  E-commerce is certainly a new development which has got a long way to go before the rate of development slows down. Much of where it will go is as yet unknown. Thus, you have to look at any investment in terms of its long-range future. Despite all the hype which accompanied the start-ups at the beginning of the twenty-first century, the likelihood of making short-term profits is low.

> **KEY CONCEPT**
>
> E-commerce is not a short-term tactic, but a strategic investment.

- *Sell products that are easy to identify.* In fact, also despite all the hype, the Internet is not – as yet – very good at explaining the complexities of sophisticated products. You have to keep your messages simple and design your website in such a way that it is easy to follow. Accordingly, this is also where existing businesses, with their strong brands identities, can win.

- *Capitalise on the value of product extensions.* Much of the hype has been about new start-ups, yet much of the success so far has come from organisations which have taken existing, very well-known and in particular well-branded products or services and put them on the Internet. Product extension gets round many of the problems of identity that bedevil new start-ups on the Internet.

> **KEY CONCEPT**
>
> Clearly identifiable product extensions into e-commerce are most likely to succeed.

- *Services that are understandable.* Much the same as simple products, this again repeats the 'keep it simple stupid' message!

E-commerce categories

In terms of the main e-commerce sectors, activities are currently split in just two directions, between consumer and business sectors:

	BUSINESS	CONSUMER
BUSINESS	**B2B (EDI)** General Motors/Ford etc + B2Employee	**B2C** Charles Schwab (Stockbroker) Amazon Dell
CONSUMER	**C2B** Priceline (Airline Tickets)	**C2C** EBay (Auctions) QXL

Figure 2.1: Consumer and business sectors of e-commerce

Of the resulting four quadrants, the two most important are currently those driven by business interests: B2B (business-to-business) and B2C (business-to-consumer).

> **KEY CONCEPT**
>
> B2C and B2B are currently the most important e-commerce categories.

However, there can be many other sectors and, in order to illustrate the range of functions to which an 'e' can be added, I will quickly list a few of the others that are being suggested as subsets:

- *e-auction* – this is a way for consumers or businesses to come together, electronically, to get involved in either bidding for offerings put forward by other organisations, such as that run by eBay, or procurement – putting their own requirements out to tender.
- *e-banking* – we also have seen some activity here; though, considering the potential numbers involved, so far

relatively few banks have allowed their consumers to access their banking activities over the Internet. The paucity of trail-blazers here is surprising because banking, now being all about electronic numbers rather than about cash, is an ideal candidate for remote working. Egg (http://new.egg.com) is one of the new online banks.

- *e-directories* – we have already seen a number of 'search engines' turning themselves into portals in order to offer a much wider range of services. The downside of this has been that they now distort their searches to promote the products they themselves offer, thus undermining the function they originally offered. If you should ever want to find the best value in airline tickets you will now be very lucky to get past the search engine's own travel shop!

- *e-engineering* – one rather special category is e-engineering, which, with the development of computer-aided design (CAD) means that various engineering processes can be linked together, not just within a company but across a range of companies, with the designs and control procedures transmitted through standardised interfaces.

- *e-gambling* – this is not much talked about, but is still significant. If you live in an area where gambling is illegal it's very easy to move offshore and gamble on one of these websites. Similarly, e-pornography is another consumer product available on the Internet which polite society pretends does not exist!

Later we will explore in more detail some other uses of the Internet, for example e-learning, the education and training systems available, and also such elements as *Enterprise Resource Management* (ERM) and *Electronic Data Interchange* (EDI) which are at the heart of B2B.

Most of this book will, however, focus on the two main sectors, business-to-consumer (B2C) and business-to-business

(B2B) which are, so far, the most important sectors in terms of e-commerce. But as we progress though the rest of the book you should remember that almost any activity can be transacted across the web. In this context, the two main sectors can also be seen as an illustration of the two ends of the spectrum – with many other different variations possible between them.

 Vital questions and answers

To end this chapter, ask yourself if your business is:

- in the business-to-consumer (B2C) sector?
- in business-to-business (B2B)?
- in a more specialised sector?

Genuine customer partnership: customer relationship management (CRM)

Overview

The most important factor driving marketing developments in e-commerce is not really a function of the technological advances at all. Except, that is, the interactive nature of the Internet allows full rein to a development which was already taking place: that of Customer Relationship Management (CRM). The main objective of this chapter is, therefore, to show you how CRM can best be applied in the context of e-marketing.

Traditional marketing theory has tended to focus on the single transaction at one point in time. Over recent years a number of people have pointed out that, in fact,

CONTINUED . . . **Overview**

what is much more important is the relationship over time, covering a number of purchases. Indeed, in most markets the profits made by organisations come from follow-on orders rather than initial orders yet, all too often, their efforts go into making that initial sale, and very little effort is put into retaining subsequent business.

The prime objective of this chapter is, therefore, to explore the development of CRM in general; and of e-commerce CRM in particular, as the ultimate expression of this. Its focus is on consumer behaviour and how this may be allowed for in your marketing activities. En route, we will also look at the changes in society, such as individual empowerment, which are leading to new marketing approaches, such as individual lifestyle segmentation, that capitalise on the new interactions open to marketers. As the latter part of the chapter explains, however, these interactions are often mediated through groups, typically through affinity groups operating as web communities. It also examines how the resulting group relationships can best be managed.

- Customer Relationship Management (CRM)
- Models of purchase behaviour (enhanced AIUAPR)
- The complex sale
- Profiling
- Individual empowerment
- Lifestyle portfolios
- Affinity groups
- Web communities
- Commercial web organisations
- Clubs

Theoretical models of consumer behaviour

Even the one traditional model which does include the repeat purchase, that of AIUAPR below, does not stress this CRM element which is central to e-commerce:

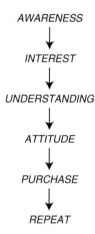

AWARENESS
↓
INTEREST
↓
UNDERSTANDING
↓
ATTITUDE
↓
PURCHASE
↓
REPEAT

- **AWARENESS** – before anything else can happen the potential customers must become aware that the product or service exists and a company's first task must be to gain the attention of the target audience.
- **INTEREST** – but it is not sufficient to grab their attention. The message must interest them and persuade them that the product or service is relevant to their needs.
- **UNDERSTANDING** – then the prospective customer must be made aware of how well the offering may meet his needs.
- **ATTITUDES** – only if the message persuades the prospective customer to adopt a positive attitude towards the product or service will she purchase it.
- **PURCHASE** – even so, the final buying decision may take place some time later, when the prospective buyer tries to find a shop which stocks the product.

- **REPEAT PURCHASE** – in most cases, this first purchase is best viewed as just a trial purchase. Only if the experience is a success for the customer will it be turned into repeat purchases.

 ## Vital questions and answers

- Does your organisation recognise that these separate stages can apply to its own marketing activities?
- Does it organise its marketing activities to allow for this?

This is probably the most comprehensive model used by many practitioners. Indeed, in traditional markets, this simple theory was rarely taken any further – not even to look at the series of transactions which such repeat purchasing implies. It was only

> **KEY CONCEPT**
>
> The purchase decision is influenced by the experience gained from previous purchases.

at the end of the 1990s that Customer Relationship Management (CRM) became more generally accepted. Inherent in this new approach is the idea that the consumer's growing experience over a number of such transactions should be recognised as the determining factor in subsequent purchases. All the succeeding transactions are, thus, *interdependent* – and the overall decision-making process may accordingly be much more complex than allowed for by most models.

As usual in the case of management fads, most organisations only paid lip service to the concept of CRM – '. . . of course we have always maintained a good working relationship with our customers . . .'. Having put it in their company report, they rarely did anything positive about it!

Some academics, especially those led by Grönroos in Sweden, did take this concept seriously, and there are a number of approaches to CRM which have been published.

> **KEY CONCEPT**
>
> Members of the customer's peer group wield significant influence.

A more practical model of purchasing behaviour

In order not to confuse traditional brand marketers too much, however, our own model[4] is built on an enhanced version of the AIUAPR model. It takes the single dimension of the original model, where it is implicit that there is a growing involvement of the customer with the product or service from top to bottom, and formalises this process. More important in the context of e-commerce, it adds two further dimensions. The first specifically reflects, on one side, the attempts by the *vendor* to influence this process – which were hidden in the original model. It shows the way in which the vendor's involvement changes from advertising at the start of the process to the highest quality support at the end – a progression which is not fully described in less complex models. On the other side, though, it also shows the involvement of the *customer* with his *peer group*, whose influence is not even hinted at in the original version. The progressive stages in this new process are shown in Figure 3.1.

The starting point is, in this case, earlier than in the original model:

- **SUSCEPTIBILITY** – even before you can build awareness, the consumer's mind has to have been opened

---

[4] Mercer, D. (1998) *Marketing for Managers*, London, Orion.

Enhanced AIUAPR

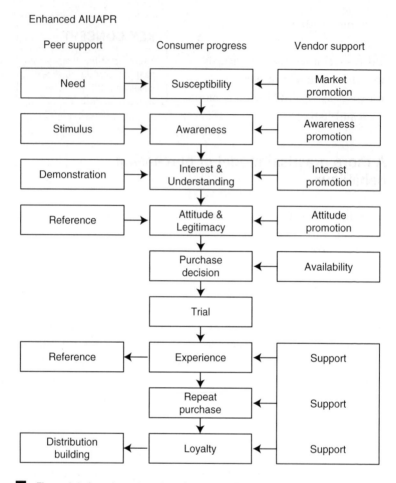

Figure 3.1: An enhanced version of the AIUAPR model

up to the concept behind the product or service. Research evidence suggest that this may have initially emerged from the workings of the opinion leaders in the consumer's peer group, rather than directly from media advertising. This is where the supplier has to accept some form of market (or segment) building role. It makes use of public relations as much as advertising. This is where many of the early e-commerce start-ups made their first, often fatal, errors. They assumed that everyone was as enthusiastic about their offering as they were, when in reality few of their prospective customers had even accepted the original idea! Thus, Boo.com, an online fashion retailer and one of the early dot.com casualties, did not seem to investigate if customers would buy fashion items without being able to try them on before they set up their site.

- **AWARENESS** – you have already seen how this works in the original model although there the role of high impact advertising (or prospecting in industrial markets) was implicit rather than being a formal part of the model as it is here. The main difference is that research shows that the stimulus is once more as likely to come from opinion leaders in the peer group. These offer a hidden, and potentially very powerful, 'sales force' on behalf of the product or service. Luckily, once you have attracted the attention of these peer group leaders, you can use the profiling on your website to induct them into their specialised role – which can be very different to that of other customers. This is an approach which was not possible in traditional markets – and is where e-commerce can make major advances! As is often the case, however, such approaches have rarely been applied – although Amazon, which is as we will see throughout the book the leader in many fields of e-commerce, does try to use its existing customer base to bring in new recruits; and America Online (AOL) puts considerable effort into building its membership base.

- **INTEREST/UNDERSTANDING** – these two are coupled, since it is difficult to conceive of one happening without the other being involved, although they may offer very different challenges to the advertiser. Again, however, it is members of the peer group, already users, who may be most likely to be able to proffer the 'demonstration' of the product (or the results of the service) to prospective consumers. In the case of e-commerce, this 'demonstration' will be through your website – so yet another part of this site should be given over to such 'demonstrator' potential (and the peer group-leaders taught how to use it). Again, this is where e-commerce scores over traditional approaches, at least in terms of allowing some control of this element which is otherwise beyond the vendor's influence. Boo.com did at least try to show what its fashion clothes might look like on a 3D simulation of the customer – but this took so long to download (up to 30 minutes) that users logged off before the image was complete! Few other sites even try.

- **ATTITUDE/LEGITIMACY** – although one further stage is added, that of 'legitimacy' (persuading the prospective purchaser that, backed by his or her favourable attitudes, a purchase may be justified), this is merged with the attitude building process; and both may be dependent on the 'reference' support from members of the peer group, who are already loyal users, as much as traditional advertising. In the case of e-commerce, the other members of the 'club' may be brought in to add the necessary legitimacy – they will be much more powerful than any celebrity presenter used in an advertisement. As already mentioned, AOL and Amazon try to give their customers the feel of belonging to a club.

- **PURCHASE DECISION** – this should be, by this stage of the process, almost automatic. For once, in traditional markets, the consumer is usually alone in making this particular decision. In e-commerce markets, some support – in the form of purchase support tools such as comparators (against competitive products), configurators (such as Dell uses to allow customers to build their own personalised PC), or pricing estimators – can be made available. Again, this support, at a critical time, is only available from an e-commerce approach. Another key element, also featured in the original model but often (wrongly) taken for granted in conventional markets, where availability depends upon the different members of the distribution chain working perfectly together, is that the product or service must be easily available for the consumer to achieve that purchase. An e-commerce vendor, on the other hand, can be in control of the whole process. Even if the product is out of stock, the customer can be given a delivery date.

- **EXPERIENCE** – one stage ignored by the original model is that when the consumer tries the product or service for the first time. This may or may not be a favourable experience, but it still represents a major discontinuity in the model. At this point the nature of the accompanying processes changes. In the case of the vendor's promotional activities the emphasis switches abruptly from recruitment to support (perhaps still involving some advertising support, but mainly in terms of conventional support services). This is perhaps best illustrated by the switch from new account selling before to account management afterwards, in face to face selling. At the same time the consumer switches from being a recipient of advice to one who can, from experience, give advice to her peer group. This should be of a positive nature, since a bad experience is typically reported to many more peers than a good one! Again, however, this different element must be provided by the website, and the 'navigation' to the new role supported. Amazon's use of customers' 'reviews' of the books it stocks, is one successful example of customer involvement.

- **REPEAT PURCHASE** – in this development of the original model this becomes almost a technicality in conventional markets. In the case of e-commerce, however, continuous reinforcement – at a very low per

capita cost – is quite possible, and better ensures
continuing loyalty. Again, the club membership employed
by AOL is a good example of this.

- **LOYALTY** – more important still is the final step, that of
  creating a loyal user, based upon successive positive
  experiences. These can be backed by sound customer
  support – for example, through the related elements of
  the website. These loyal users become, in turn, the
  'references' for new users (or even the 'opinion leaders'
  who feature so strongly in this enhanced model). This is at
  the heart of the 'club' approach to e-commerce direct
  marketing.

 ## Vital questions and answers

- Which of these stages does your organisation
  address?
- Does it recognise the role of peer-group leaders?
- Does it invest in building loyalty?
- What is the 'asset' value lost if such loyalty is not
  maintained?

The seemingly distinct steps listed
above often, indeed usually, overlap. Thus, some sections of the
population – the opinion leaders,
say – could be well into the repeat
purchasing stage while other
sections are only just beginning to
perceive the need. Accordingly,
promotion and advertising often will have to meet the
requirements of a number of stages at the same time – a
complex demand, which is one reason why very successful

KEY CONCEPT

Unlike those dependent on
the mass media, e-com-
merce customers can
choose the messages which
suit their current needs.

advertising campaigns are so rare in traditional markets! As we have seen, though, the flexibility of websites should allow this to become routine in e-commerce. Not least, the customer can self-select the promotional support which is relevant to him – and the stage he is at in the purchasing process – something which is not possible with media advertising. *This is a major change in Customer Relationship Management.*

Looking at the problem from the viewpoint of traditional vendors, the first, one-off, end of the spectrum may be termed *transaction marketing* – and it's often suggested that most consumer goods companies are at this end of the spectrum. On the other hand, it is believed that business-to-business is much more at the other end of the spectrum, relying upon *extended relationships*. In fact, both sectors should maintain the relationship because it leads to optimal profits.

One, perhaps unexpected but not wholly unrelated, feature of 'audience behaviour' was reported by Leon Festinger.[5] It was described by him as *cognitive dissonance*: '. . . interest in all forms of promotion, particularly of advertising, reaches a maximum after the consumer has made his or her purchase.' The usual explanation for this apparently illogical behaviour is that the consumer is then searching for the proof that will justify their recent decision. In looking at the competitive advertising, say, the consumer is trying to seek out its flaws, in comparison with the chosen product or service, in order to obtain reassurance that his decision was the correct one.

The importance from the vendor's point of view is that advertising still has a job to do even after the sale has been made! In addition, the messages needed to address cognitive

[5] Festinger, L.A. (1957) *A Theory of Cognitive Dissonance*, California, Stanford University Press.

dissonance may be subtly different –
for example, where they are needed
to provide reassurance – and should
take account of the fact that these
purchasers will also represent the
main source of future sales, as well as

> **KEY CONCEPT**
>
> A vendor's promotional activities should not end with the purchase.

serving as peer group references. This is another area where
the comprehensive nature of the website allows this task to be
taken on – and targeted – at the same time as the other
promotional messages are being delivered elsewhere.

Differences in Internet purchasing behaviour

We are told, much of the time, that e-commerce is very
different from traditional sales. But then – as we have seen –
people proceed to describe the related purchasing behaviour
in very much the same terms as for traditional markets.
Indeed, much of it is the same – that is the message of much
of this book! But there may still be some significant
differences in the detail; and these differences will now be
discussed.

Impulse purchases and rebuys

There is good reason to believe that
impulse purchases may be much less
significant over the web. People
have to take a deliberate decision to
go to a particular website, and even
within that website to go to a
particular product or service. There

> **KEY CONCEPT**
>
> E-commerce may be more effective in terms of rebuys rather than impulse purchases.

is, accordingly, nothing – apart perhaps from the banner ads
– which might induce them to make an impulse purchase.
This will be bad news for the many retailers whose

merchandising ability is often designed precisely to persuade people to make impulse purchases. As you wander through a well-merchandised high street store, your eye is drawn to any special offers, and often it is those special offers which the retailer, and the vendor, need to make their profit. This is much less likely to happen with the web.

The problem of trust, and in particular of touch (you can't touch a product on the web or even see the sort of people who will provide the service) is one that means that the initial purchase also may be made through more traditional routes. Associated with this, though, there may be significant information seeking, known as 'infoseeking', as people use the web to compare manufacturers' stories. This is something that is much more difficult without the web – although this will not console the website owners who still do not supply that initial purchase! People like to walk up and down the high street, laying their hands on the product they want to buy, to see if it is substantially made and won't fall apart in their hands!

However, once the initial purchase has been made, then their rebuy can safely be made over the web, and – with some searching – at the most attractive price. By then trust in the product is established. Then, a website may be used to capitalise on what has gone before.

One peculiar outcome may be that the initial buy will be under the control of those who invest in both clicks and mortar, those who have traditional channels in addition to the Internet – and the pure Internet suppliers may be locked out. It may also mean that the traditional suppliers do all the hard work and make the investment in the initial sale (which is often unprofitable), for Internet suppliers to meet the rebuy market, where the profit is maximised.

> **KEY CONCEPT**
> ___
>
> Clicks and mortar vendors may gain the best of both worlds.

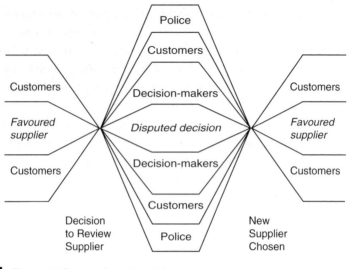

Figure 3.2: The complex sale model

The complex sale

On the other hand, the complexity of the changing influences in a business-to-business (complex) sale over time can be shown in Figure 3.2.

Here, in the period of the 'disputed decision' when the supplier is changing, there are three main groups involved:

- *Customers* – these are the people who actually use the product or service and who, for most of the time, are the main contact with the supplier.
- *Decision-makers* – those in authority who have the formal responsibility for making decisions, and who may be quite separate from the customers.
- *Police* – the various departments (such as purchasing and quality control) who can veto the decision if certain standards (such as price limits or quality levels) are not met.

Vital questions and answers

- Who are the key (purchasing) decision-makers in your own organisation?
- Who are the 'police' in your own organisation?

Figure 3.2 over-stresses the time devoted to such decision-making. For most of the time, probably more than 90% of the total, the winner of the disputed purchase decision becomes the 'favoured supplier'. It then proceeds to deal only with the 'customers' in the diagram above, usually the direct customers or end users who make use of the product or service; and, most importantly, has no serious challengers over long periods of time. That is, until something undermines the customer's confidence in the arrangement. This is usually as a result of a significant failure on the part of the supplier and hence the emphasis, elsewhere in this book, on customer opinion tracking and complaints handling. Then, as shown above, the more complex – decision-making – phase is entered.

As CEO of a large PC dealership, I was eventually worn down by the excellent (hard-selling) pitches made by a very capable representative of one of the major computer manufacturers. As I was in the market for adding an extra line, I eventually

KEY CONCEPT

Customers rarely consider changing a supplier unless you damage the relationship.

agreed to stock his offering. When, over the next few months however, his service levels were found to be wanting – he was too busy closing other new dealerships – I destocked the line, at some cost. It was a totally unnecessary loss for him, since just a little effort would have ensured we would have continued to make sales for him of several hundred thousand dollars a year! The moral is that you should never allow your customers to start wondering whether you really do deserve the 'favoured supplier' tag.

The customers, in this context usually the users of the product or service, typically are the real decision-makers; the formal decision-maker generally has no option but to support their decision. Indeed, it is very unusual for permission to be refused – unless it is controversial, or especially important, or cannot be resourced. But always waiting to pounce are the 'police'. These are the individuals (or departments) with veto power which, if brought into play, may outweigh even substantial amounts of customer protest (hence their considerable leverage, which may go far beyond their apparent power in the organisation). They may accordingly sometimes become an unexpected stumbling block; even a minor resource decision is likely to be policed by the finance department, not the formal decision-maker. You should be aware, though, that there are many other forms of police waiting to see if you overstep the mark (sometimes 'secret police' whose involvement you do not even know about until they veto your pet project). These may range from experts checking the technical specifications to those charged with guarding labour practices. The rule is, accordingly, that the widest possible range of customer contacts should be made. They may turn out to be the secret police themselves (or they may be able to warn you who these are). If you recognise who they are it is often easy to defuse potential problems with them in advance, but rarely so easy after the event. Accordingly, in a given sales situation, the more people you can recruit to your side from the group who will decide or influence (or police) the purchase decision, the higher become your chances of winning that decision (and the safer your position). Once again, the website has an important contribution to make, in terms of influencing these 'police' who would rarely make a personal approach to your organisation, but will happily become infoseekers on your website.

There is much theory, and even more opinion, expressed about how the various 'decision-makers' and 'influencers' (those who can only influence, not decide, the final decision) interact. Thus, decisions are frequently taken by *groups*, rather than individuals. Often the official 'buyer' does not have authority to take the decision. An important aspect of the organisational buying process, in particular, is therefore the balance of influence between these various actors. E-commerce adds the important element that – via the website – the vendor can to a certain extent be involved in their decisions.

In this way, the most important aspect of handling the complex sale may be understanding how a *partnership* can be built; finding out how the customer's organisation can, in effect, be fused with your own. Shared elements of identity or values, shared group member-

> **KEY CONCEPT**
>
> You must identify who are the customers and who are the decision-makers – and the 'police' – but above all you must build a genuine partnership.

ship, or simply shared business interests are often what makes such partnerships work; and the emphasis here is on *shared*. It is important to recognise these synergistic components, which often revolve around intangible elements (such as the organisational cultures or even – with more volatility – personal relationships between the key participants). Again, the e-commerce website can be a powerful device for maintaining this feeling of partnership over time, and it is not dependent on a salesperson's irregular calls, or the tender mercies of an ill-informed outbound call centre!

Customer relationship management and the Internet

In all these contexts, probably the main (commercial) benefit of the Internet and the web is *enhancement of the relationship with the customer.* This is partly because of the opportunity for communication. You, or at least your computer, can talk interactively with individual customers on a regular basis. This is something that was never possible before. Even in business-to-business marketing this level of interactive, ongoing, conversation was limited to the most important customers; to the top 20% highlighted by the 80:20 rule. Now something similar can be extended to many of the customers in the bottom 80% of a market. In mass consumer markets vendors can also now build relationships with individuals, or small groups of individuals, where previously they had to conduct their market research on the basis of averages and could only advertise, through the mass media, to very large segments of population. In a different context, I hold face-to-face meetings with a dozen or so members of my main research group, but also talk to the more than 600 others who contribute through an e-mail conference!

Profiling

Sophisticated use of the Internet, along with equally sophisticated use of database technology, means that it is possible to track profiles of individual customers. This is the sort thing that Amazon (www.amazon.co.uk) does

> **KEY CONCEPT**
>
> Active profiling helps to build a relationship with an individual.

very well at the moment – it knows what sort of book you buy and tailors its promotions to that profile. That is a very potent ability for any marketer to tap into.

On the other hand, this probably isn't about the web as we now know it. That is essentially a 'pull' offering, whereby people will visit you only when *they* want to. To be in control you need to have much more *direct* technology, which is currently e-mail. Paradoxically, the rules for running this sort of business come from direct mail. For some time this has been viewed as almost beneath contempt by most marketers. This may be reasonable, considering the amount of junk mail we all receive, but the problems come not from *successful* direct mail activities but from the unsuccessful ones. The lessons to learn, as we will see later, are those in which direct mail has been shown to work.

At the heart of these is the steady build-up of *trust* – so that these customers feel not simply that you can be trusted, but that you have something to give them.

 Vital questions and answers

■ Does your organisation employ such profiling of its customers?
■ If so, how?

The limitations of the Internet for customer relationship management

Not everything is perfect, though. The first limitation is simply the numbers involved. As with any new technology, penetration is limited. At the moment, probably more than two-thirds of the population do not even have Internet access. That means, for many organisations, the core of their business will have to remain based on their traditional approaches, with the Internet as an add-on. This may also mean that the businesses with the greatest advantage in the early stages might be those which rely on 'trickle-down' from the wealthier members of the population. In fact, there is very little evidence of this having been the case. If anything, the new entrants to the e-commerce markets have employed a shotgun effect, which may be one reason for their difficulties!

One of the leading advertising agencies, with some relish, tells the apparently true story of not just one but a number of early start-ups which, when asked by the agency to describe the 'product' they would be required to advertise, replied by asking, 'What do you think it should be?'

With the third of the market that do have Internet access, there is probably a problem of *usage*. You don't just want to contact people who have the IT equipment in their home, you want them to be *using* it – and using it for the purpose of transacting business, as business-to-business or consumer buying, in the office or their home. This cultural problem may take longer to resolve.

One of the less well-known observations, in usage of communications technology, is that there is a 60:40 effect. Below 60% penetration, the potential customers have to mix their Internet business with their traditional

> **KEY CONCEPT**
>
> Usage rapidly accelerates once a 60% penetration level has been reached in a customer group.

business – and conventional business will always take the lead. This was certainly true with early e-mail communications in the office. As I found, when I was commissioning IBM's first fully 'electronic' office building in Europe, below 60% penetration most people started with the normal written/ typed memo, and only then grudgingly converted this into an e-mail. On the other hand, once the 60% figure had been passed, everything flipped. Then people started to treat the electronic element as the natural part and switched to that as their prime means of communication. The change then was very rapid, moving from 60% to 100% very quickly indeed – as those not on the e-mail list fought to get on it, otherwise they were cut out of the communication paths. Much the same can be expected to happen with e-commerce. The problem is that, with only 30% penetration currently, we are still some considerable way off that magic 60%.

Vital questions and answers

- Has this level yet been reached *within* your organisation?
- Has this level yet been reached *with your customer contacts?*

Customer service levels

One of the most important aspects of customer or client service is that the 'product' or 'service' should be available when and where the customer wants it. If it is not available, an immediate sale may well be lost. More important, long-term sales may also have been lost if the customer is forced to change to another brand, and then decides to stay with that brand. In view of the 'immediacy' of e-commerce, this is even more important in this field and is especially important in terms of retaining the customer's loyalty. If delivery promises are broken, as apparently they are as much as two-thirds of the time in e-commerce, then it is hardly surprising that customer loyalty is at best frail in this sector. This is another lesson that Amazon (one of the few which does generally meet its delivery promises) has learned – but at a very high cost (in spending billions of dollars setting up its own delivery chain)! In the UK, Tesco quickly gained more than half the online grocery business by investing heavily in a new fleet of dedicated delivery vans – whilst using its existing stores to supply the products to these.

The percentage availability is described as the service level. It might seem that the simple answer would be to achieve 100% availability. The problem is that, even for e-commerce – where stocks held by suppliers can often be added into the equation – the cost of achieving these service levels rises very steeply as it approaches 100% (Figure 3.3).

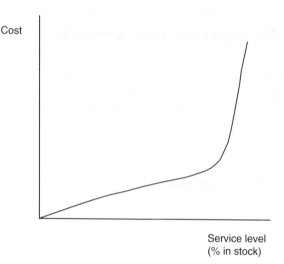

Figure 3.3: The cost of achieving service levels rises as it approaches 100%

There is a very clear trade-off here between customer service (level) and cost. Fortunately, the indications are that, in terms of demand generated, customers are not significantly affected by minor variations if there are generally high levels of availability (Figure 3.4).

There are, however, other elements of customer service level. Some of these relate to the time it takes to meet an order (where, unlike the situation described earlier, the product is not delivered 'ex-stock'). This is called the 'lead-time' (or sometimes the 'order cycle time'). Clearly, the shorter the lead-time the better the service.

On the other hand, it is frequently the case that the *reliability* of the lead-time is more important than the time itself. Thus, a customer who has to arrange a number of other activities to mesh in with the delivery of the product – for example, a new carpet – will often prefer that the delivery date is certain, albeit at a later date, rather

KEY CONCEPT

Reliability in delivery is often more important than reduced delivery times.

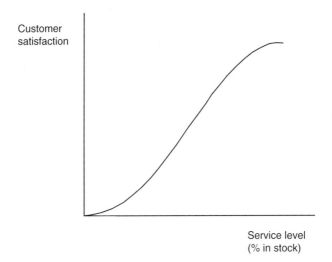

Figure 3.4: Customer satisfaction rises in line with stock levels

than it being uncertain at an earlier one (when the other elements of the customer's operation – in our simple case, the carpet fitter – may be kept waiting until the delivery actually occurs!). This is also a matter of trust. If Amazon says it will take four to six weeks to supply a book, rather than the normal two or three days, you will probably accept the delay – assuming, usually correctly, that the book is in short supply. But should you be promised two days instead, and it actually takes two weeks, you will write off that supplier – probably for ever!

Vital questions and answers

■ How reliable are the delivery promises of your own organisation: 75 + % are achieved, 50% or less than 50%?

A subsidiary, but important, element is how long (the response time) it takes a customer to find out what is actually happening to the order!

Queuing

In the specific context of queues associated with provision of a traditional service, David Maister[6] lists a number of 'proportions', the principles behind which have wider applicability:

1 Unoccupied time feels longer than occupied time.
2 Pre-process waits feel longer than in-process waits.
3 Anxiety makes waits seem longer.
4 Uncertain waits are longer than known, finite waits.
5 Unexplained waits are longer than explained waits.
6 Unfair waits are longer than equitable waits.
7 The more valuable the service the longer the customer will wait.
8 Solo waits feel longer than group waits.

I suspect that his points about the psychology of queuing will probably tap a rich vein of your own personal experience! All of them, with the exception of the last, are just as applicable to e-commerce. In fact, they are even more important, for

> **KEY CONCEPT**
>
> E-commerce customers expect responses in a matter of seconds.

there is no reason why electronic communication with a computer should not be undertaken almost instantly. Where

[6] Maister, D.H. (1988) The psychology of waiting lines. In *Managing Services: Marketing, Operations and Human Resources*, London, Prentice-Hall.

people are willing to queue in a shop for a few minutes, they are often unwilling to queue for your computer for as many seconds – as Boo.com (which expected its customers to wait for up to 30 minutes) found to its cost. These are all reasonably well known principles, yet how often have you known a management – apart from that at Amazon – that has taken notice of them?

 PAUSE FOR THOUGHT

■ The only exercise I would suggest at this stage is to go to the website of your own organisation and see what the response times are like. But do this from home.

Do not do this on the internal network – that will work at the speed of light – do it from home and see what your customers themselves experience. It is one of the most common features of IT support staff that they only ever work with fast (internal) network links to the servers, and never experience the frustrations their incompetent process designs impose on customers!

Individual empowerment

Although we like to talk about e-commerce being the major force at large in the world, in fact there are other forces which may be just as powerful but not as obvious. Thus individual empowerment, a social force, may have just as great an indirect impact. It also may have a direct impact, as one of the other drivers which are shaping the future of e-commerce.

Individual empowerment is about the personal ability of individuals to gain access to, and implement, their own rights without having to go through the groups to which they belong. This is something which will be familiar to all those who have studied the future of the Internet, and in particular its one-to-one relationships. Over previous decades individuals' rights may have been 'published' but access has been controlled and censored by groups. In the UK, for example, it was by the classes to which they belonged or, even worse, to which they had been allocated. The great strength of the Internet is the peer-equalising nature of its one-to-one content, and of course its discreet anarchy. This doesn't mean that one individual can use the Internet to change the world. But it does mean that the individual will be able to *participate* in the process as of right, without the censorship which has limited his power in previous centuries. In this context, the Internet may be a genuinely revolutionary development – and e-commerce may be at the leading edge of that revolution. Its e-shoppers are, in many ways, the unlikely new revolutionaries – as those organisations which fall foul of them soon realise! Not least, the pressure groups – from Greenpeace members destroying GM crops, to transport activists blockading fuel depots – have shown what may be achieved by positive action when co-ordinated through new electronic communications!

However, the particular way e-commerce, and the Internet, will be most important will probably be in terms of releasing individual talents – allowing people to fulfil their true potential. Previously, where they have had to work through groups,

> **KEY CONCEPT**
>
> Individual empowerment will both release people's true potential and revolutionise some markets.

they could go no further than the group allowed. Now they can use the Internet to do what they like and, more importantly, become what they want.

PAUSE FOR THOUGHT

- Do you feel that the impact of pressure groups has increased over recent years?
- Do you personally feel that your *own* 'rights' have been enhanced over recent years?
- How have these changes improved your position (at work and/or in your private life)?
- Do you think that the Internet has given you more power to deal with organisations?

Portfolios of lifestyles

In this context, one of most important short-term elements is the development of lifestyles. In marketing we have long acknowledged the existence of lifestyles, and its importance, through the VALS^{TM} set of lifestyle measures. Thus people – for the purposes of marketing – can be assigned to a number of different lifestyle categories.

It has been claimed that such lifestyles are already over-taking the class categorisations as the best way of grouping individuals. In fact, the takeover has not been as rapid as many people believed. This is probably because the new lifestyle groupings can be almost as arbitrary as the old class-based ones are now. The key new lifestyle development is therefore that individuals can now *choose* their own unique lifestyles. Lifestyles are not bought off-the-shelf with Adidas trainers or their Gap jeans, but include a whole range of decisions about activities, and values, as much as the products they buy.

One interesting development is that people – having established their lifestyle, which may be totally different from what might be expected from their class and even from the (VALS^{TM}) lifestyle categories – are going beyond this to build a *portfolio of lifestyles*. In this way they put together all the trappings of a lifestyle, much as one might put together an outfit for an autumn day and put it in their wardrobe. They pull it out when the circumstances dictate that it is suitable. Within the same wardrobe they may have a number of other lifestyles, which they pull out to meet the requirements of other situations. Thus you may have the financial analyst who still wears a suit to work in the morning, but in the afternoon wears combat clothes for a protest about foxhunting and then in the evening puts on his party best for attendance at a rave, with its associated drugs scene. In the old days such different lifestyles would have been mutually exclusive. Now they can be switched from moment to moment almost like articles of clothing.

The important aspect, from the viewpoint of e-commerce, is that the web is an ideal way of delivering these lifestyles. It doesn't just include products, though offering a catalogue of the various products will help an

> **KEY CONCEPT**
>
> The web is an ideal vehicle for delivering new lifestyles.

individual to select what is needed for each lifestyle, but also contains knowledge and activities – along with values – which may also be relevant to each of these lifestyles. So creating your portfolio of lifestyles is rather like going to a cookbook and selecting the various ingredients. The web is an ideal place to find those ingredients and even to access them or purchase them. What you do with them, or how you cook the final dish, is up to the individual – and that is why individual lifestyles are so different and so fascinating.

 Vital Questions and Answers

- Does your organisation take account of customer 'lifestyles' in its marketing activities?
- If so, how?

If you want to see some examples of the new 'lifestyles' on offer, go to the website for the Royal Society for the Protection of Birds (RSPB), at http://www.rspb.org.uk/, currently the largest affinity group in the UK, or that of Greenpeace (http://www.greenpeace.org/) or Amnesty International (http://www.amnesty.org/); and see what their members demand.

Lifestyle segmentation

This lifestyle segmentation, on a *one-by-one* basis, is very new. It obviously can't use all the sophistication of factor and cluster analysis that we have previously used for segmenting

> **KEY CONCEPT**
>
> The web can deliver *truly* individual lifestyles.

groups. On the other hand it doesn't need this, because it doesn't need to identify who belongs to the group – it only needs to identify, on its database, the profile of one *individual* consumer. This is no trivial matter, where you are handling many millions of customers. Thus, one of the great benefits claimed for loyalty programmes, when the superstores first embarked upon them, was that it would enable them to record the profiles of their individual customers – and then use these profiles to market to the individual. That hasn't happened yet, although the benefit could be significant. The main reason that it hasn't happened is quite simply the problem of manipulating such vast amounts of data, and taking meaningful decisions on the basis of the outcome. What may be critically important for the web, therefore, is the concept of *rule-based marketing*. In this approach, you don't decide the specific activity for a group of customers, as you might when using conventional segmentation; instead, you set up various rules which decide what the activity will be depending upon the specific profile that emerges for the individual. Thus you may not segment your target audience by age or class, but you may say very simply, as did Sears Roebuck in its department stores, if this customer bought a refrigerator a year ago and didn't take out a warranty with it, then let's contact them and try to sell it again. That is easy to do for a single transaction to a single customer, but the problem comes when you try to do this across the board; where the superstore may have 50,000 lines and a quarter of a million customers.

 PAUSE FOR THOUGHT

■ I will not ask if you undertake any one-to-one marketing; as you will have gathered, that is very unlikely to be the case as yet. But, what would be the implications for your organisation if you were able to do this?

Permission marketing

One of the new buzz phrases in marketing is 'permission marketing'. Within the context of e-commerce, it is a genuinely important concept. Much of marketing management views the target audience as literally a target to be aimed at, whether they like it or not. Permission marketing quite simply says that the result of this conventional targeting is not merely that much of your effort is wasted on people who aren't interested in your message, but that it may positively alienate a significant proportion of them. This is particularly true of junk mail and especially of junk *e-mail*. The answer is simply to get the permission of these prospective customers. You just ask them for the right to talk to them! But be careful, this does not mean that they will buy your product, it just means that they will let you talk. They may not even listen, but at least you have established that they are not averse to the conversation. Again this is a very potent marketing development. It means that, compared with a normal sales situation, the customer has stopped in their tracks and is *listening* to you.

It also means that, as in the conventional (face-to-face) sales situation, the first thing you should then do is ask them a question – not try to sell a product. This again requires some quite sophisticated marketing, and – even more important – some quite sophisticated changes in marketing attitudes.

> **KEY CONCEPT**
>
> Trust is built by asking customers for their permission to 'talk' to them.

Web communities

Groups of customers also have a place in this new e-commerce environment. The interaction with members of such groups, and between members of the groups, will be important, not least in achieving scale advantage in a one-to-one environment. This is also the area where we move from theory, which is well founded in traditional marketing, to totally new experiences – and that poses some considerable uncertainty about the outcomes.

When you talk about these new communities, what is implicit is that they share some feature or other – otherwise we wouldn't even be able to identify them. But this is a new form of group segmentation, which may be even more powerful than traditional segmentation, even though it may not be as powerful as the *one-by-one segmentation* that we have already talked about.

These new communities have one great practical virtue, and that is that they segment themselves. They are not so dispersed through the rest of the

> **KEY CONCEPT**
>
> Web communities which are peer groups, often mediate individuals' purchasing behaviour; but they are usually very easily identifiable.

population, or at least in terms of their links through the web they aren't, but they see themselves – and link themselves together – as a single community. What that community is based on is entirely up to them. It may be that they make up a car owners club, which may be of considerable interest to car manufacturers, or that they are the University of the Third Age, which may be a considerable interest to education providers but also to financial services providers.

The first starting point for such communities will probably be existing user groups and conferences, which tend to be linked by the technology rather than by the culture. This may be a much less powerful motivation, but at least you know that the technology is there for you to communicate with them!

 Vital questions and answers

- What, if any, web communities do your e-commerce customers belong to?

Affinity groups

On the other hand, what is slowly emerging is the grouping together of individuals in what are best described as *affinity groups*. They come together because they share some cultural interest or affinity. They, in particular, share interests outside the new technology. This makes them potentially very valuable, possibly the most valuable groups of people for their suppliers. They may share a love of one composer's music or they may be interested in birds – the Royal Society for the Protection of Birds is the largest affinity group in the UK. Equally they may have more indirect links – my own Open University has two and a half million alumni, who are linked only by having been through a similar form of education. That education may have encompassed science or arts or languages, but is not easily seen as a shared interest. On the other hand, these people do have a shared culture. They are well-educated and they share certain cultural aspirations, all of which may well be of interest to a wide group of vendors. They are likely to have higher incomes than most, and will probably be interested in some leading-edge cultural products and services – so, again, you can see that they may be very attractive to certain groups of vendors.

The most potent form of group for the individual may be those *self-help groups* which set out to help each other with certain activities. The strength of the Internet in this context is that it can bring together people from all round the world. Although it is worth emphasising that, at this point in time, the best group working takes place, paradoxically, not between those who are remote – and couldn't meet in any other way – but between those who regularly meet face-to-face!

> **KEY CONCEPT**
>
> Affinity groups may offer the most valuable markets in the longer term.

In another manifestation of the process, there are many tens of thousands of newsgroups around who share information about a very wide range of topics. At present these are very much social groupings, as are all those I'm talking about.

 ## Vital questions and answers

■ Are there any specific affinity groups to which your customers belong? If so, how might you reach them?

Consumer-to-consumer (C2C) communities

The big unknown is how the new online communities will work together. As yet, even these affinity groups have not really gelled. The conferences, the bulletin boards, have really been little more than another form of e-mail communication. Thus, the members have really only been sending letters to each other – as they might have done in the past through the clubs they belonged to.

However, these groups could potentially be very valuable in terms of doing business with each other. It is probably best to consider these in terms of an example. So, let's briefly look at the example of a model railway enthusiast.

This enthusiast may live almost anywhere in the world, but let's say – for the sake of argument – he lives somewhere in the Highlands of Scotland. With the Internet at his command he could be anywhere. In building his model train layout, which could be massive since he has an old barn as the room in which to build it (so maybe there is some logic to setting this in the Highlands!), he may well want to take on the concept of a route through the Rockies in Canada. Accordingly he can get round his ignorance of all things Canadian by talking to his counterparts in that country, to one or several of them, to start to build up an idea of layouts. At the same time, he can get some background history so that he can later illustrate his talks about the layout with some genuine historical details. Having got the layouts sorted out, he can then get advice, from around the world, as to how he may create the model features needed. He may also search the world for suitable suppliers, for the rolling stock and for the model buildings which he will locate in his miniature landscape. He can then order these various items, which may be delivered by local suppliers or may be sent by airmail from around the world. When he has finished all of this – which may take several years – he can proudly provide pictures of this, even moving pictures, to anyone from around the world who wants to look at it. He may then also be able to offer his expertise, which he gained during the project, to other enthusiasts around the world.

There are two important points here. The first of these is that the enthusiast is dealing with individuals and organisations who are located anywhere in the world. The second – which we haven't mentioned so far – is that he may well become involved in commercial transactions

> **KEY CONCEPT**
>
> Individual members of some groups may be distributed globally, with e-commerce providing the only vehicle for marketing to them.

while doing this. He will certainly have to pay the suppliers of the materials (the rolling stock for example), as usual. But he may well also have to pay his Canadian contacts for the research they are doing, or perhaps for the copies of the layouts which these people have already produced. But, equally, having finished the work, he may well be able to sell his own expertise – and maybe even some items of newly designed rolling stock, in return. This latter part indicates the potential. There are a significant number of transactions involved in this example, which may be typical of a whole range of commercialised hobbies, and although individually these might be relatively small, together they can add up to a substantial sum – such layouts can cost many thousands of pounds.

It should also indicate the problems of trying to forecast what form this particular type of e-commerce might take, and especially how its economics might work. In essence, its form is totally flexible. It is typically a bilateral relationship – possibly a multilateral one – where the few people involved decide what they want to do together, what services they want to offer each other, and negotiate some form of price for these (probably around some form of price list).

This indicates the potential for consumer-to-consumer markets, but unfortunately does not indicate how these may develop.

Web organisations: portals

We now come to the other side of the coin, the offerings which target affinity groups. So far *portals*, the website owners who will offer entry to the web for their members, have been organised very generally – the classic example is AOL, whose only shared cultural thrust seems to be that of popular entertainment.

But it is easy to see that, as competition grows, these portals may ultimately have to become more focused. Thus *horizontal portals*, which tend to dominate at the moment, will

> **KEY CONCEPT**
>
> Horizontal portals aspire to be one-stop shops.

probably continue to try to be all things to all people – to be a 'one-stop shop'. Freeserve (www.freeserve.com) is one such example. As competition increases, their focus still may not be on developing a special range of offerings. Instead, they may still aim to be the ultimate one-stop shop, but they may specialise in the *groups that they appeal to* – at one extreme, they may choose to appeal to everyone as AOL tries to, or at the other they might just appeal to Open University alumni.

There are also the *vertical portals*. Amazon is the classic vertical portal, a site dealing only in books (or at least that was what it did originally – now it is trying to become a one-stop shop

> **KEY CONCEPT**
>
> Vertical portals aim to be specialists.

as well (and that may be one of its problems)). The advantage of such vertical portals, over horizontal ones, is that they have a very clear identity which can be easily communicated to their target market. As it originally existed, you knew exactly what Amazon was there to do. The fact that it is now not so clear may well have weakened its position – and its brand.

Clubs

More fundamentally, based on the previous experience with direct marketing, one of the most powerful approaches is the club – which has very strong links to its members.

> **KEY CONCEPT**
>
> Clubs have strong links with their members.

In the face-to-face environment some clubs, such as the gentlemen's clubs in the West End of London, can be very powerful indeed. Others, such as the Automobile Association, or even the Royal Society for the Protection of Birds, have a much looser control over the loyalty of their members. But they do still have recognisable mechanisms for interfacing with members, and such a mechanism – as evidenced by the sale of the UK Automobile Association – can become a commercial one, and ultimately a very valuable one.

Moderating these groups

One new skill needed will be that of managing the links between members of these groups. In particular, it will be necessary to develop the skill of creating links between various member groups, as well as within the groups themselves. The first aspect of this may well be establishing the *characteristics of the group*, why it exists, and hence what structures are needed to manage it. This is very different to normal customer relationship management, and may well require some form of sophisticated computer modelling, possibly based on artificial intelligence, if it is to be applied across the many groups which are emerging.

As we saw earlier, the profiles of individual customers pose significant problems of data warehousing and data mining to get their details out from those data warehouses. The problem becomes even more complex where you are also trying to monitor relationships *between* those customers. Clearly, there has to be some way of handling this, but as yet it is not obvious how this will come about. If you know of one you may be on your way to becoming the next e-billionaire!

Vital questions and answers

- How do you organise your customer contacts (e-commerce or otherwise) to handle 'networking' issues?

Global hide and seek

CHAPTER 4

Overview

The first objective of this chapter is to show you how
the individual customer may be tracked, and a profile of
their 'buying behaviour' created. Even so, the most
important 'device' for making the sale may simply be a
sound website (process) design. If your visitor can't find
what they want, they won't buy it! FAQs (Frequently
Asked Questions) are one approach, but an understanding of the whole process of interaction with
customers and of their related behaviour (especially in
terms of repeat purchase rather than initial buy) may be
productive. In particular, this chapter looks at how
services pose different challenges to products.

- Customer identification
- Navigation
- FAQs
- Purchasing behaviour
- Service factors

Tracking users

Inherent in many of these approaches is the concept of
tracking the user. You will profile them and follow them as

they work their way through your web offering. This is the best market research for tailoring your site to individual profiles. Until you know customers' purchase behaviour, which may often be much more important (and much easier to determine) than their social characteristics, you really haven't got a grasp on your customers.

User identification

Thus, the owners of websites need to be able to identify visitors when they return – not least so they can personalise their responses, as Amazon for instance does. To do this they need to track some unique identifier. Unfortunately this cannot simply be the user's web address, since this may be shared with other users – and, in any case, this is lost if it comes through a proxy server (as is often the case with a popular site).

There are a number of ways customers can be tracked. Daniel Amor[7] lists some of the main approaches:

> **KEY CONCEPT**
>
> A key to successful e-commerce is identifying, and then tracking, visitors to your site(s).

 GETTING STARTED

- *Cookie* – this is placed on the customer's computer and is retrieved when the user logs on the next time.
- *Basic authentication* – where users identify themselves through a login and password.
- *Domain name* – they can sometimes be identified through their domain name.
- *IP address* – or by their IP address.

---

[7] Amor, D. (2000) *The e-business (R)Evolution: Living and working in an interconnecting world*, NJ, Prentice-Hall.

- *Personalised URLs* – they can also use personalised URLs, one for each authorised user.
- *Strong authentication* – finally, some form of digital certificate – issued by the vendor or a third party – may be used.

Vital questions and answers

- Which of these, if any, do you use?
- Which might you use in future?
- What implications might this have for your e-commerce processes?

As you can see, one common solution is to place a 'cookie' on the visitor's hard disk. This is a file which the operating system allows external websites to create, and which contains information about the users that the external site owner wants to store – it

KEY CONCEPT

Cookies are currently the most effective way of tracking visitors to your site.

is a unique identifier which links the user to the site's database. The simplest form is one which links the user to a single site, as Amazon does – .amazon.com.Userid = 12345 (for instance) – which then is used to link to the main Amazon database containing all the details of the user's prior purchases. A more complex, and ethically much more questionable, approach is to place a cookie on the user's hard disk on behalf of an agency. The cookie is recognised by other websites who use it to tailor their advertisements.

Navigation design

Getting customers to enter your site is only the first step. Once the customer is there you must make it easy for her to move around the site and get the information she wants. Clearly there must be some promotional content to this, you will want to – as far as possible – control what she is doing, in order that you can steer her to making a purchase. On the other hand, you should realise that with the new empowerment of the individual you have to be very careful. People are now well aware of what vendors, especially those on the web, are trying to do. If they think that you are trying to manipulate them they will run a mile. Worst of all, if sites try to keep users in, as some websites do, and won't allow users to get out (by deliberately disabling the Back button of their browers), they will flee a site and never come back again. Nobody likes to feel trapped.

More generally, an especially important aspect of web design is that of the *processes* deployed by the website; and in particular those relating to the way customers navigate around it. Above all, the navigation support tools should reflect how customers *naturally* want to get around the site; so watch them to see what they *want* to do.

> **KEY CONCEPT**
>
> If you want them to do business with you, it must be easy for customers to find their way around your site.

If you need any encouragement, Jim Sterne[8] reported that 'In April 1998, Shelley Taylor & Associates announced the results of a study of the world's largest 100 companies. The results included the fact that only 42% of the sites incorporated global navigation, only 22% used subsection navigation, and only 33% had site maps.' Things may have improved since then; but make certain your own site does not fall into this trap.

[8] Sterne, J. (1999) *World Wide Web Marketing*, second edition, New York, Wiley.

PAUSE FOR THOUGHT

- A useful exercise is, from time to time (as its design changes), to make a visit to your own website(s) and see how easy it is to find your way around. Once again, do this from home rather than on the fast network in the office. Even better, get a friend who does not know what to expect to do the same. You may be surprised, and even shocked, at what they have to say!

Interaction

Perhaps the most important part of a website is that it should interact with the customer – this, after all, is the great benefit that e-commerce is supposed to offer! Thus, at every stage, what should be encouraged is *interaction*. In much of marketing, what customers say to you is more important than what you say to them. You are there to sell products, no doubt, but they may well be there for a much wider experience. Just being faced with a catalogue of your products may do little for them. It may do even less when, as some suppliers do, the list is organised by product number without any obvious structure telling you how these differ.

Some of the earlier website 'feed-back' may have been based upon form-filling, but you should *always* provide an e-mail address (preferably linked direct to a 'reply' button) so users can talk to you free of restrictions. More important, make sure that you reply to all such emails within a matter of hours, if not minutes. Nothing loses potential customers faster than the feeling you don't care. For the same reason, also give a phone number. This may seem to go against the

> **KEY CONCEPT**
>
> The more your site interacts with customers the better it will perform.

spirit of the Internet, but it means they can harry you if the email *isn't* answered; and you really should want to know if your systems are failing! Indeed, give them every address – snail mail as well – up to that of your CEO so they can get through to somebody – no matter how hard your staff try to stop them!

To create extra interest which may bring customers back to the site, however, conventional advice is to put lots of other pieces of information on the website. You should make it so interesting that people want to come

> **KEY CONCEPT**
>
> Make it easy for them to contact you, even by phone if necessary.

back time and time again – for the interest offered by the site itself. So you should create user clubs (where users can exchange information), provide topical articles (which relate to the use of your product or service, say), along with articles by experts (including your own staff), support bulletin boards (where customers can put up messages for other users), or offer entertainment (computer games, etc.). Don't get too carried away with this, however, for – unless you are charging in some way for them being on your website – you shouldn't lose sight of the fact that at the end of the day you want them to buy something. Indeed, the more you offer, the greater the chance they may get lost. Customers may love that, but you won't make a profit out of it.

 Vital questions and answers

- Based on the visit to your own website which you just completed, how would you rate its interest value: good, adequate, poor, or irrelevant?
- How did your friend rate it: good, adequate, poor, or irrelevant?

FAQs

As a footnote to this section, one of the things that is most useful on many websites is a list of Frequently Asked Questions (FAQs). This, in many respects, is a substitute for face-to-face contact. When people e-mail you directly, asking specific

> **KEY CONCEPT**
>
> FAQs provide good support for customers, prior to the stage when they can only resolve a problem by personal contact.

questions, you answer the emails with the best help your technical team can provide – though many organisations don't get this far, but *you then keep that answer* (along with the original question) and you put it on the database. Customers can then – when they have a similar query – see if it has already been answered.

This means, of course, that you have to have a good database with a viable way of enquiring on it. It is just as bad to have 10,000 FAQs with no obvious route to the one the customer needs as to have none at all. It also means that those answers have to be concise and up-to-date – both of which demand significant staffing resources. On the other hand, it offloads many of the routine queries which would otherwise have to be handled face-to-face, and – above all – it really is appreciated by customers, who are used to it taking days for their answers to come back through more conventional channels. The BBC (www.bbc.co.uk) makes good use of FAQs.

Vital questions and answers

- Do you provide FAQs?

Inner marketing

Marketing is, by definition, primarily concerned with the world outside the organisation. On the other hand, if it is to optimise the use of the resources, it also has to be concerned with what lies inside the organisational perimeter. This is known as *inner marketing*. It is an even more important concept for e-commerce – not least as an antidote to your staff's remoteness from the customer.

Increasingly, the most valuable resource of any organisation (and particularly those in the service sector) is its people; and the skills they possess. In tapping this internal resource, so that the organisation can face up to its external environment and in particular to its unseen

> **KEY CONCEPT**
>
> To provide the best possible service, your staff should also have been sold on the ideas you are promoting.

customers, it turns out that many of the traditional tools of marketing can be used to great effect in the very important areas of internal communication and motivation.

In the 1990s such campaigns tended to focus on Total Quality Management (TQM), on the basis that the overall quality that the customer perceives comes from every part of the organisation – from support and administration staff just as much as from the workers (or the robots) on the production lines. 'Inner marketing' is in many ways therefore the ultimate extension of TQM in that it fixes 'quality' exclusively in terms of the marketing context (of what is important to the customer) *for every employee.*

In a similar vein, many organisations in the service sector, and some in the manufacturing sector – though surprisingly few in e-commerce – have 'customer service programmes'. These use many of the promotional devices of marketing – advertising, incentives, seminars, etc. – to persuade employ-ees (particularly those in contact with customers) to adopt the correct attitude to those customers. Such campaigns have received a mixed response. The problem has often been that the management implementing them are themselves unconvinced of the message they are trying to send; and it is unrealistic, under these circumstances, to expect the employees to react more favourably than the management itself. Probably the most frequent shortcoming is that such campaigns are run as very short-term programmes, which everyone knows they can ignore, since the next month will be bound to bring a new campaign.

In this context, *inner marketing* is a powerful concept. It says quite simply that employees should be 'marketed' to in exactly the same way as customers.

Implicit in this concept (which should not be confused with the internal market) is that all aspects of marketing should be incorporated. In particular, a 'dialogue' should take place – 'inner marketing' is as much about finding out what the employees want as persuading them to do what the organisation wants!

> **KEY CONCEPT**
>
> Internal marketing can be as valuable to promotional programmes as that to the customer.

The first requirement, and the one therefore which distinguishes it from almost all other 'customer service programmes', is some form of *marketing research*, exactly as with traditional customer marketing programmes – but here conducted on the organisation's own employees! This should be used to determine where they stand, for example, in relation to their perception of the customer (Is the customer seen as friend or foe?) and of the customer service programmes which are likely to be the main focus of the research (Does anyone do anything more than pay lip service to them? Why?). Furthermore, as with any piece of sound research, it should also attempt to find out where employees might wish to stand in the future; exploring their attitudes and motivations (Do they really want to offer a good service? If not, why not? How can they be persuaded to change their views?). The outcome of this is most productively described as consensus, since this best incorporates the attitude of mind which should lie behind it – the search should be positively designed to find the outcomes, especially in terms of values, to which all the participants (in this context, most importantly, members of staff at all levels, but also the managers and customers who will also have to accept these values) will be able to commit themselves.

As already suggested, this is even more important in e-commerce operations. The staff there may have even less contact with customers – and may come to focus on the technology rather than on the human impact of their work. When I complained to a senior manager of an IT multinational, one which I normally respect and which has an excellent reputation for service, about the very real problems with its (technical support) helpdesk operation, he made it clear that he thought the problem must lie with me rather than them; after all, they had spent many millions of pounds on the software which had replaced the people! This was despite the fact that, as a personal friend, he knew that I have worked in IT for more than three decades – and can programme in a dozen different languages. What hope is there for mere mortals?

Vital questions and answers

- Does your organisation conduct any research into the opinions of its own staff?
- If it did, what unwelcome news do you think it might find?

Internal opinion surveys

Internal research may have great benefits. Such 'opinion surveys' are remarkably effective devices for obtaining information on the inner market. If applied regularly to all staff, they are also remarkably good motivators and contributors to a positive culture. At the peak of IBM's power, one of its most powerful tools in developing its justly famed relationship with its staff was the 'opinion survey'. Every two years, every IBM employee took part in an anonymous survey of how they felt about IBM and what it was doing, as well as how they felt about their immediate management. This was, since the results were published, a remarkably powerful device for ensuring that managers took note of their subordinates' opinions! The results were (very publicly) acted upon, to the benefit of the 'inner market' – not least because the employees (unlike those in most other organisations) recognised that IBM was listening to them. Unfortunately, remarkably few other managers use such surveys.

Only with this basic information on employee attitudes (however derived) can the 'inner marketer' start to devise the programmes necessary to create the new attitudes, the conviction in the goals handed down to them, which will deliver the

> **KEY CONCEPT**
>
> Internal opinion surveys can discover the problems holding back service levels.

requisite service to the external customers. The actions needed to achieve the end result follow the familiar path of any marketing campaign, although they are alien to much of human resource management. Even in the marketing context, it should be recognised that it may take far longer to achieve the desired results than in a traditional consumer marketing campaign – for the requirement frequently is to make fundamental shifts in attitude.

At the most basic level, staff will need to understand what is expected of them, by their own management and, in particular, by their customers. It is remarkable how many 'improvements' in customer service are advertised to the customers but never explained to the employees who are to deliver them, let alone agreed with those employees. Beyond this, the essence of any marketing campaign, as with any military one, is that all the actions happen at the right time, and in the manner planned. The inner marketing campaign is essential (whether it is formally or informally implemented) to ensure this happens. How many times have you heard of, or even experienced, offers advertised by retailers which their branch staff deny exist? How many times have you found yourself talking to a 'call-centre' and begun to understand that the reputation of these new institutions – as the sweatshops of the Western world – is fully evidenced by the lack of motivation by all involved?

 Vital questions and answers

- I will not ask you to find out whether your organisation has an *effective* opinion survey process. If you work in any of the handful of organisations which do this you will be very well aware, from your own positive experiences with it, that this is employed. But what impact do you think implementing such a survey might have on your organisation?

Managed suggestions

One especially powerful technique lies at the heart of Japanese techniques; and, indeed, at the heart of Toyota's success. This was developed by the American Philip Crosby, but adopted by the Japanese rather than US corporations, as the eleventh step of his famous 14-step 'zero defects' programme. In the original, as developed for the Pershing missile programme in the US, it was titled 'Error Cause Removal (ECR)'. This eminently forgettable title may be why it *has* been forgotten by the West! Toyota, however, retitled it – confusingly for the outside world – as their 'Suggestions Scheme'. Like the Western version, the idea is that any employee puts a suggestion into the nearest suggestion box as soon as he or she recognises a problem which needs solving; and they are then rewarded for this observation (Toyota receives more than two million suggestions each year, and implements more than 90% of them). The crucial difference from the Western equivalent is that the employee is only required to identify the problem, and need not suggest a solution (which is the main thrust of Western schemes, and it is the *solution* there which justifies the payment). The problem is then passed to the relevant management, and it is their task to find a solution. To distinguish between the two, I call this process 'Managed Suggestions'.

This is both the simplest and the most powerful technique in inner marketing. It may sound like a trivial process, but identification of the problem (the correct question to ask) is usually the most difficult part of problem solving. The Crosby approach directly addresses this difficulty, and ensures that the problem is captured immediately it is identified. This technique, orginally proposed for use in quality improvement, can be used in a wide range of situations (ranging from JIT (just in time) to customer complaints). It is, at the same time, one of the simplest techniques (it could be implemented, in theory at least, in any company in a matter of days), and one of the most powerful.

Its one inherent limitation is that it can be too successful, too soon. It can pose impossible demands on managers who are unprepared to deal with the problems thus unearthed. How many managers could respond effectively to each worker under their control generating dozens of 'suggestions' a year? That the benefit only comes after the manager has identified the solution is bad enough, as is the demoralisation of the managers faced with a massive backlog of suggestions, but the demoralisation of the workers whose suggestions are not being dealt with is even worse. Thus, in practice, this simple technique can only be used by an organisation which has already implemented many of the other techniques (typically those problem-solving techniques used by Japanese corporations) and whose managers are already conditioned to meet its demands. Crosby deliberately waits until later in his overall programme, typically until more than a year after the start, to introduce it. In order to cope with the demands imposed by a managed suggestions scheme, the management must have already been trained in many of the 'Japanese' problem-solving techniques. On the other hand, an e-commerce extension to an existing business might be expected to face a rather less complex set of activities than its parent – and 'managed suggestions' might be a much easier tool to implement!

One obvious extension to the concept, which the Internet makes feasible, is to use a similar process with your customers! Ask them, too, for their suggestions.

The inner marketing bonus

An important fact to note here is that the process also includes the lowering of customers' expectations, as experience brings home the truth of what they may realistically expect. In many situations, it is the customers' expectations which are steadily adjusted downwards (without any improvement of the staff positions) until their view accords with the lower levels on offer. The thicker line in

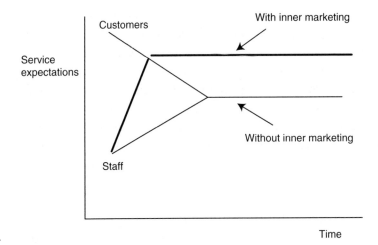

Figure 4.1: Inner marketing improves staff response to service expectations

Figure 4.1 shows what might be achieved with the application of inner marketing to positively improve the response rate of staff. The end result is that the final level of perception is significantly higher, potentially offering a major competitive advantage.

The techniques here may often be closer to those of education – and, indeed, may revolve around significant amounts of retraining. The service offered to customers, for instance, is in many cases only as good as the skills available to provide it; and those skills often need developing.

Culture

Some years ago, Peters and Waterman[9] stressed that the resulting 'culture' of an organisation (generally speaking, the common values shared by its employees – whether developed

---

[9]   Peters, T.J. and Waterman, R.H. (1982) *In Search of Excellence*, London, Harper & Row.

positively by management as suggested here or by default) can be a very important contributor to its success. Even though Tom Peters is no longer the guru he once was, and most of the examples he chose have long since lost their lustre, such 'culture' can still be important in determining what 'customer service' is provided – even in e-commerce. Thus, the 'culture' of the company is often what conditions 'customer service'. IBM – as one supreme example – maintained a philosophy of 'customer service' throughout the whole company (applying to all employees) as its only marketing objective for more than half a century, with spectacularly successful results (and an equally spectacular disaster when it abandoned it). Both McDonalds and Disney have similarly strong cultures, and it shows (not least in their spotlessly clean premises – but also in their bottom-line profits).

The problem of addressing the 'cultural dimension', even though this is an essential element which must be allowed for in any marketing operation, is normally that of time. Changes in the culture of an existing

> **KEY CONCEPT**
>
> Don't underestimate the time it takes to change organisational cultures.

organisation may take years to be completed. If existing cultures are strong, and the changes are major, the process may take decades. Both IBM and Japanese corporations, who probably have the strongest cultures of all, needed up to fifteen years to fully develop all the detailed aspects of the new, and rich, cultures they were introducing. Culture is not, therefore, a topic to be taken lightly, although more minor changes (particularly those which complement the existing culture – and characterise the earlier conviction and commitment stages) may be accepted more rapidly.

The saving grace for the e-commerce start-ups is that the creation of a new culture can, on the other hand, be a matter of months, not years. Even the clicks and mortar operators may be able to create a new ethos in their own 'start-ups' relatively rapidly – if they are deliberately separated from the main business (though that, of course, will pose another set of logistical problems!). It is especially important, therefore, that the cultural changes follow a deliberate, well thought-out, plan. If they are allowed to happen by default, while management gets on with what they think are more important things, they may get locked into a very unproductive model, which will then take seven years or more to correct!

Services in the post-industrial society

Having explained how e-customers, and their communities, may evolve, along with some of the 'products' they may demand, we can look at the range of knowledge services, in particular, around which e-commerce will increasingly revolve. As Amazon has demonstrated, physical products can be sold over the web, but even in its case its service elements are the ones which give it a competitive advantage. In general, though, it is the service industries which are gradually coming to dominate e-commerce (B2B as much as B2C).

Once more, though, the characteristics of these are very similar to those of services in conventional markets, though the balance may be quite different. So, we will now look

> **KEY CONCEPT**
>
> People are just as important within e-commerce organisations.

at the various characteristics which are often referred to as the 3Ps which, in addition to the 4Ps, give total of 7Ps for services. Though the original 4Ps have, in fact, lost their position at the leading edge of marketing theory, the 7Ps are still to a degree valid in terms of *differentiating* service industries. So starting with those parts of the list which relate to the elements of intangibility – you can't touch services, whereas you can touch a product – these are indeed rather different for e-commerce:

- *People* – the first of these Ps stands for people. Thus, for most service industries, people are the key. This is partly to deliver the service, and is just as true of a hairdresser as for a management consultant. *The 'product' in a service is most often the people involved.* This may seem to be much less true of Internet-based services in general, and of the new knowledge industries in particular. Indeed, face-to-face contact rarely occurs, but people are present in several different guises. The first of these is that they will provide the original knowledge, either as input to the general database or as specific knowledge in response to specific questions. On the other hand, they are also a necessary evil, as an integral part of the operations needed to debug problems. It is this latter aspect which most e-commerce organisations have yet to learn. They assume that, because they have spent money on the software which delivers the knowledge, they don't have to have any human interface. The reality is, as most of us know from experience, that the incidence of glitches or bugs in the software, is much higher than the designers ever allow for – and dealing with these requires very talented individuals. The level of service is, accordingly, often determined by the quality of the individual people who are on the helpline – if such a helpline even exists!

- *Place* – the new place is not the physical place which most traditional services rely on. It is, instead, the website. The old adage 'location, location, location' must be replaced by 'look to the website'. This is where the activity is. It's where the key investment has to be made, although the level of that investment will typically be much lower than that for traditional investments in real estate.

- *Promotion* – the final P stands for promotion. With
  services, the character of the service is often largely set by
  what you say about it. It, especially, is set by the branding.
  This branding is even more important for services than
  for products. A weak physical brand can occasionally be
  saved by a strong product performance, but a weak service
  brand rarely can. The brand is the service. This is even
  more true of e-commerce. The whole tone of the offering
  may be set by the brand. In particular, it may be set by the
  brand extension, since it is much easier to take a non-e-
  commerce brand and extend this offering on to the
  Internet. It is much more difficult to start up a new brand.
  This was the situation which applied to many of the
  original e-commerce start-ups. They had to spend tens of
  millions of pounds in the UK alone just trying to establish
  the brand, paradoxically spending this largely on posters
  or on bus sides, rather than on advertising across the
  Internet – which you might have thought was more
  suitable!

Beyond these three Ps are a number of other special
characteristics:

- *Inseparability* – this is one of the less obvious aspects of
  services. What this means is that the 'product', the service,
  is produced at the same time as it is consumed and both
  happen after the order is placed. This is very different to
  most conventional products which can be held in stock. It
  also means that stockholding, in the conventional sense, is
  not possible. Equally, though, it may mean that stock
  control is even more important. This is because, for
  example on an airline, the seats it has are totally
  'perishable'. When the plane takes off, if the seats aren't
  full you can't save them for sale later. Fortunately, in the
  case of e-commerce the only 'physical' resource that

matters – at least where you are selling knowledge – is raw computing power. This means that you can set up, in effect, infinite supplies and hence not lose any business in this way.

- *Ownership* – in the case of services, 'ownership' is very different to that of a product. It is much more ephemeral. Perhaps when you have a haircut you enjoy the result for a few weeks, until it grows out. But in a number of other areas, for example travelling by bus, once done it is gone. You have nothing to remind you of it – unlike with a physical product where you may have it in perpetuity. In e-commerce, of course, you can store the information that you have downloaded, for example on your hard disk, so it is still there in electronic form. But, usually, once you have the information, you don't need it again. It is a one-off transaction.

- *Variability* – this is one aspect where e-commerce is particularly different to services in general, because in conventional services the people content is subject to variability. On the other hand, computers are totally predictable. Given the right rules they will do the right thing every time.

To summarise, therefore, in comparison with the traditional characteristics of services:

- *Intangibility* – the offering becomes even more remote and even more intangible, where you don't even have the presence of staff to reassure the customer.
- *Promotion* – this is combined with place, and the website becomes the prime vehicle.
- *Branding* – is even more important than for physical products.
- *People* – should not be ignored since they can make major contributions to the success of e-commerce.

> # Vital questions and answers
>
> ■ Put the above bullet points in order (1–4) in terms of their priority to the activities of your organisation.

New marketing theories for old?

CHAPTER 5

Overview

We now move on to three chapters which, in some respects, represent the heart of the book. I have already explained that much of the marketing needed for e-commerce is exactly the same as is needed for traditional markets. Chapters 5–7, therefore, look at the various elements of the traditional marketing mix to see how they fit in with the demands of e-commerce – and how they may need to be changed.

The main objective of this chapter is therefore to look at the basics of the *marketing mix*, in the context of its extension into e-commerce, before focusing on the strategic decisions on *segmentation* and in particular on *positioning* – to cope with the e-commerce forces which compete to diffuse the product/service identity – in order to establish what needs to be achieved by the *brand strategy*.

- Marketing mix
- Marketing research
- Segmentation

CONTINUED . . . Overview

■ Positioning and position drift
■ E-commerce diffusion
■ Branding and customer franchise
■ Branding policies and the Rule of 123
■ Economies of scale and 'power diamond'
■ Leaders and followers
■ Competitor responses and history

The new marketing mix

The most fundamental statement to be made about most of e-commerce, at this point in time, is that it is just one more element to be added to the marketing mix.

This may be the opposite of what you expected. You will have already gathered, from the media hype, that a fair number of people involved in the e-commerce marketplace think that it is the *only* part of the marketing mix. That is taking too short-sighted a view of all the other elements. Even if you are looking only at new start-ups, you still have to add the product features, promotion, service support, and all the things that would normally be expected to go into the marketing mix. As always, success is dependent upon getting the marketing mix right. In some areas of e-commerce, especially where it is an extension of existing business, this balance may become increasingly important. E-commerce certainly makes a contribution and it cannot be ignored. But, at the end of the day, everything else is still there to contribute to the final mix.

If you're looking for the traditional model which can be most easily extended to e-commerce, then it is worth looking

> **KEY CONCEPT**
>
> E-commerce is just one element in the overall marketing mix.

at *direct marketing*. For a long time, direct marketing has been neglected by the academic world. It has commonly been seen by academics to be the

> ## KEY CONCEPT
>
> You can learn a great deal from conventional direct marketing.

province of cowboys. But the reality is that although it is difficult to put into theory, and that puts off academics such as myself, the features that characterise it are often close to those that now apply to e-commerce. Equally, our own research with practitioners shows that the 'rules of thumb' typically used in direct marketing – because more elegant theories are missing – are often more valuable in practice than the erudite theories of the academics! This is because they offer *practical help* which is *immediately of use* in building upon *existing skills and knowledge* to develop *specific solutions to unique problems* whilst clearly highlighting the *limitations* of the 'theory' involved. Where e-commerce is so new, and its lessons as yet uncertain, such rules of thumb – derived from what little practice there has been (and what even less success has been achieved!) – are correspondingly even more valuable.

The 'rules' may well be different in the future. Certainly the balance between them may change, but they offer a good starting point for much e-commerce marketing.

 Vital questions and answers

- How does your own organisation see e-commerce activities fitting into its existing marketing mix?
- Does it see e-commerce as requiring a totally separate marketing strategy?
- Or does it see it as an extension of the existing mix?

Selling versus marketing

Moving to another part of marketing theory, one which was the subject of much debate (in the earlier days of marketing) on the difference between selling and marketing, clearly e-commerce *must* be on the marketing side of this; though, at the beginning of the decade, the naïve promotional campaigns of many of the start-ups scarcely seemed to recognise this! One problem is that it is quite difficult to 'push' through the Internet. People will come to *buy* from you rather than expect you to go to them and *sell*. On the other hand, there still is some push technology around, for example that to serve subscribers to the financial news services, which can be treated rather like direct mail, so the picture even now is not totally clear. But, in general, e-commerce is much more like marketing rather than selling.

Marketing research

This is the traditional starting point for marketing, and there has been a great deal of talk about the Internet, and especially the web, being an excellent source of desk research. That may be true for certain purposes but, in the short term, the quality of the search engines is still too variable to guarantee success. The data that emerges is too often of questionable quality. Worse still, it is difficult to know whether the resulting data is well-founded, or the output of expert opinion, or just opinion from ill-informed individuals which may be quite useless. So one of the first things one must do, when using the Internet as a source of market information, is to decide the likely accuracy of the material.

The Internet is difficult to use for survey research, because the population frameworks are simply

> **KEY CONCEPT**
>
> Question the validity of anything you find on the web.

not there. In the population as a whole you can use electoral rolls and even telephone directories, but equivalents to those are not available on the Internet, so it is, as yet, quite difficult to select representative samples. Indeed, you should, as a matter of course, suspect the various methods of obtaining *any* sample populations used.

It is also said that the Internet is a useful device for focus group research. It is difficult, though, to see how the very sophisticated techniques normally employed in focus group research might work, since these depend upon quite close relationships – including body language – between six to eight people locked in a room together. We certainly have not been able to achieve this, although we have used the Internet extensively for the equivalent of very large-scale conferences, with several hundred people involved at a time. But, although these can be used to obtain some similar information, the dynamics of these are quite different to normal focus groups.

 Vital questions and answers

■ What market research, of any type, have you undertaken about e-commerce?

Segmentation

However, the Internet and the web should be the ultimate answer to segmentation, to the extent it should be possible to segment down to the *individual*. That possibility may not be immediately achievable in practice because – as we saw earlier – it is very difficult to manage millions of individual segments! The initial decision which matters most in segmentation is choosing the number of segments you can manage, when it is difficult enough managing just four or five segments. Everything else then falls into place, and the computer programs are then able to dimension the factors and cluster the data to produce that many segments. As was suggested earlier, it might eventually be possible to use some form of rule-based segmentation instead, to handle much larger numbers of segments, and this may well be more important in future, but as yet it is not available.

Probably the most important segmentation still is by the *benefit* the consumers seek. In other words, you should look at the history of what has happened previously and apply some form of segmentation based on usage. For example, Amazon uses previous

> **KEY CONCEPT**
>
> E-commerce can productively be used to segment down to the individual.

book purchase behaviour to categorise future promotional suggestions to its individual customers. This is a very effective technique. Besides optimising Amazon's promotional messages, users are actually grateful to Amazon for suggesting such useful books to them.

 Vital questions and answers

- Does your organisation treat e-commerce customers as if they belong to a special segment?
- Does it segment its customers within the e-commerce sector?

Positioning of existing products and drift

There can sometimes be confusion between 'segmentation' and 'positioning'; and indeed the two processes often overlap. The key difference is that *segmentation applies to the market itself,* to the customers who are clustered into the 'natural' segments which occur in that market. The *positioning relates to the product or service within the market,* and to what the supplier can do with these 'products' to best 'position' them against these segments. At the macro-level this process is, however, much the same for e-commerce as it is for conventional markets.

A further complication is that 'positioning' can sometimes be divorced from 'segmentation', in that the supplier can choose dimensions on which to position the brand that are not derived from research, but are of his or her own choosing. By default, this is typically the case for the new, stand-alone e-commerce brands. Such positioning can be applied (to differentiate a brand, for instance) even when segmentation is not found to be viable – or where the 'segment' is the individual! In practice it typically uses many of the sophisticated techniques applied to segmentation, but in its simplest application it only requires that you decide 'where' you want your product or service to be against the critical dimensions (or variables) which are applied by its market/customers.

> ### KEY CONCEPT
>
> Segmentation applies to the market itself, and positioning relates to the product or services within the market.

Easiest of all to use at the macro-level are graphical 'maps' which show the position(s) against these dimensions. Conventionally, such *product positioning maps* (sometimes described as 'product space') are drawn with their axes dividing the map into four quadrants. This is because most of the parameters upon which they are based usually range from 'high' to 'low' or from ' + ' to ' – ' (with the 'average', or mean, or zero position in the centre, where these axes cross). This is best shown by a typical example in Figure 5.1.

In Figure 5.1 there are just two clusters of consumers, one buying mainly on the basis of price (and accepting the lower

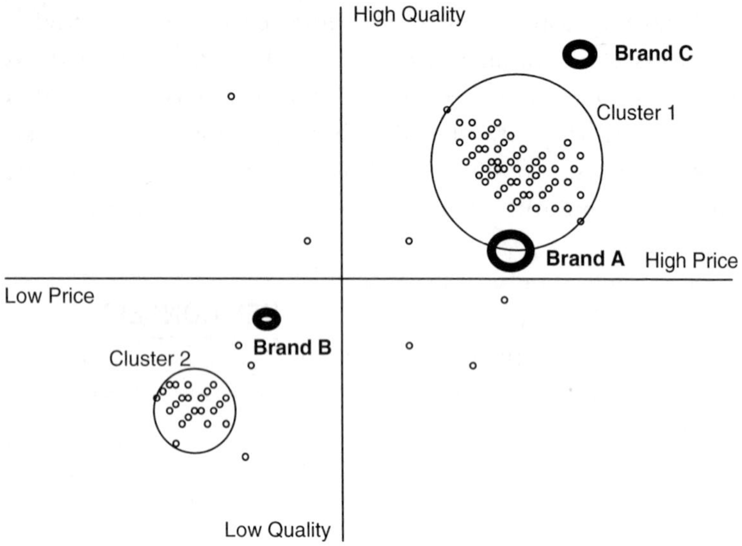

High Quality

Brand C

Cluster 1

Low Price

Brand A   High Price

Cluster 2   Brand B

Low Quality

Figure 5.1: A product positioning map

quality this policy entails) and one on the basis of quality (who are prepared to pay extra for this). Against these segments there are just two main brands (A and B), each associated with a cluster or segment. There is also a smaller brand (C), associated with cluster 1, offering an even higher quality alternative (but at an even higher price).

Real-life product positioning maps will, of course, be more complex, involving a number of such dimensions, and they will be drawn with less certainty as to where the boundaries might be. But they do, once more, offer an immediate picture of where potential may lie, and which products or services are best placed to tap this. They also offer a sound basis for 'repositioning' existing products, or launching a complementary new product as a brand is

KEY CONCEPT

Positioning maps are essential for repositioning exercises.

extended into e-commerce, so that they better match the requirements of the specific 'clusters' on which they are targeted. In Figure 5.1, Brand C might be content to remain a 'niche product' product. Alternatively, the positioning map shows that if it were reduced in price slightly (and backed by sufficient promotion) it might become a very competitive contender for Brand A's market share.

In most markets – even before the advent of e-commerce – customer requirements change over time, perhaps due to social (or fashion) factors or – perhaps more likely – to technological changes, such as the Internet, in the market. These changes may be relatively slow for long-established brands or very rapid for some fashion products; and fastest of all for developments in e-commerce. It is imperative, therefore, that you develop your existing products in line with these changing requirements. This is just as true for long-established brands as new ones, although – because the changes are slow – there is a danger that these new requirements are overlooked. It is, of course, even more important in the case of e-commerce, where the pace of such change can be fast and furious. If you do not develop existing brands in a regular and rigorous manner you may find yourself the victim of 'position drift'.

Figure 5.2 shows an even simpler example of a *positioning map*.

You can, once more, use this map to position your brand as close to the ideal as is possible for the segment(s) you wish to address (and hopefully dominate). The problem is that this shows only a *static* picture. Over time, position drift can significantly change the picture. In traditional markets, as well as e-commerce, this may come about for four main reasons:

1 Consumer drift
    As consumer tastes change, the segment (cluster) that contains them will shift its position. Its centre of gravity

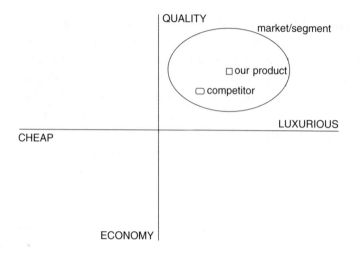

Figure 5.2: A simple positioning map

will move, and its size may change as consumers switch to other, perhaps newer, segments. As the e-commerce elements in the marketing mix grow, the clusters may shift significantly (Figure 5.3).

The position of your brand *relative* to the ideal position, within this cluster, will reflect this drift.

2 Competitor drift

Alternatively, your competitors may shift their positions – so that your own relative position, your competitive advantage, may become less than optimal (Figure 5.4). In the case of entry into e-commerce, the effective mix of competitors may also change.

This may pose a particular problem if you are trying to target several segments – including some in e-commerce markets – with just one brand, since any move to respond

Figure 5.3: Consumer drift

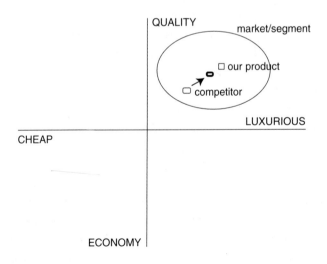

Figure 5.4: Competitor drift

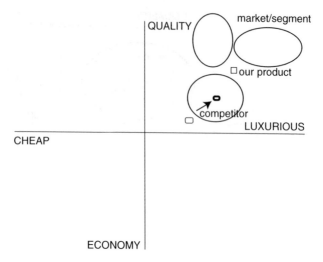

Figure 5.5: Another example of competitor drift

to a competitive threat in one segment may leave the rest of the segments exposed.

Much the same problem may, as we will see below, occur in e-commerce, where the brand position is diffused and diluted by one-to-one marketing which targets individual customers across the market.

3   Ego drift

Perhaps the most common drift of all, however, occurs where 'brand managers' (or their advertising agencies) *gratuitously reposition their own brand in a less optimal location.* This is usually justified on the basis that consumers are bored with the existing messages, and an exciting new approach is needed, but it is also a common response to an extension into e-commerce. The real reason is often that members of the management team, frequently persuaded by an agency creative team itching to make their own distinctive mark, are bored, or are confused by what they believe are the very different requirements of e-commerce – which, as we have seen, is usually *not* the case.

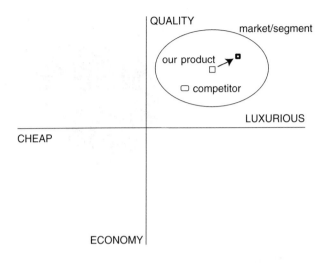

Figure 5.6: Ego drift

4 E-commerce diffusion drift
   In the e-commerce sector, drift
   is inherent, as the one-to-one
   element – at the heart of
   effective customer profiling –
   is pulled, by the differing
   needs of the individual
   customers, away from the core positioning set by the
   overall brand (and its advertising). Thus the starting
   position shown in segment 1 in Figure 5.7 can easily
   become diffused, as in segment 2, to a much less
   competitive position.

KEY CONCEPT

Individual e-commerce positions may be pulled by many different forces.

The challenge here is to balance a *clear public identity* with the *private one implicit in the growing relationship* with the individual customer. The winning brands will probably be those that publicly encapsulate general values which can also be focused on the individual needs at the private level.

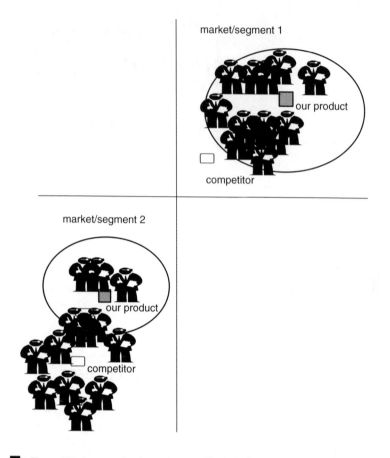

Figure 5.7: An example of e-commerce diffusion drift

The biggest problem caused by any of these types of drift, even that of e-commerce, is that it usually occurs so slowly that it is not noticed by the brand manager – in the timescales that he works to, even in e-commerce, the changes are imperceptible. It is for this reason that, as a result of position drift, brand positioning maps must be updated regularly (*very* regularly in the case of e-commerce), and the changes plotted as accurately as possible, so that the trajectory of any drift may be determined, and corrected.

Vital questions and answers

- The practical exercise I would suggest here is simply to update the positioning maps you should already have, to take full account of your e-commerce intentions. This may be quite time consuming, but the insights you may gain should be the most valuable you will gain from the work in this book.

Competition

The 1990s were the era of unbridled competition – the subject then of almost as much hype as e-commerce has received recently! Politicians and the academics preached this, and much blood was spilt between organisations competing on a price basis. This is one area where it is arguable that the positions should be very different for e-commerce, though it is worth stating that so far price competition has been just as vicious, and it has been disastrous for many new entrants. But that was probably for the same reason as price competition almost destroyed the PC market some time ago. Where a new entrant has nothing else to offer, as was the case with too many of the start-ups, undercutting competitors' prices was the only way they knew of winning some soft business. It was less easy for them to see that in so doing they might have been building up substantial losses, as indeed happened.

The point about competition in e-commerce is that, at least if you look at the competition theory of the 1990s, the situation should be much less dire. Thus the evidence from conventional markets is that competition is cut-throat when there are only three to five competitors of

> **KEY CONCEPT**
>
> In theory, e-commerce should be less competitive, at least in terms of price-cutting, than it actually is.

similar size fighting for the brand leader advantage. If the predictions are true, there will be many hundreds of competitors fighting for the same position on the Internet and – counter-intuitively – that should ameliorate the position somewhat.

Economies of scale

At the same time one of the main justifications for fighting for conventional markets share was that the extra sales allowed economies of scale to be achieved. The extra volume generated by such competition enabled the winning vendors to have lower costs, often significantly lower costs, which then justified the original price-cutting moves. This principle lay at the heart of much of the work of Michael Porter, who was the guru of 'competition' in the 1990s.

Although it is often claimed that it is able to reduce costs overall, it is not obvious that there are really *significant* economies of scale on the Internet. The difference in the operating costs between a corner

> **KEY CONCEPT**
>
> Traditional economies of scale may *not* apply to many e-commerce markets.

shop and a multinational are not anywhere near as dramatic, as they are using other delivery methods. Similarly, the control of distribution channels and the imposition of legislative barriers, competitive devices often used by the large multinationals, do not work to anywhere near the same effect in e-commerce. Finally, the problems of overcapacity, which have often driven price-cutting by organisations desperate to recover their overheads, should be less likely to apply in e-commerce. The investment in capacity, in terms of hardware anyway, is relatively minimal. On the other hand, ill-judged investments in advertising and promotion of some of the more naïve start-ups trying to build market share may still result in similarly unwelcome outcomes.

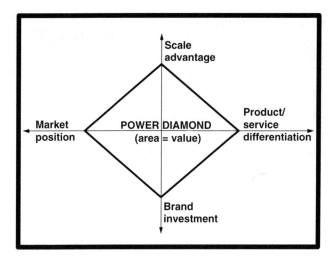

Figure 5.8: The power diamond

Simplifying matters somewhat, but not quite as much as Michael Porter did, I would suggest that competitive power – across the whole of marketing, but especially in e-commerce – can be built on four main fronts, which make up the 'power diamond' seen in Figure 5.8.

Two of the factors, 'differentiation' and 'scale advantage', are those which are also at the heart of Michael Porter's work. The other two, 'market position' and 'brand investment' (or, from the other side of the relationship, 'customer franchise') are not usually considered in competition theory. It is the total area between these (which reflects the overall power of the brand), and how the cutting edges (the corners of the diamond) are deployed in practice, which indicate how much competitive leverage the brand may be able to generate.

In e-commerce, as I have already said, 'scale advantage' is much less important, and – in the conventional (Michael Porter) sense – so is 'differentiation', which can often be copied in a matter of days, not minutes.

This leaves the other two, 'market position' and 'brand investment', which he does not include in his equivalent theory, as being the key determinants of competitive success in the new environment, and we have explored these already. The important point to note here is that the rules for e-commerce may be quite different. Positioning and branding may be even more important than price – or even the product!

You will appreciate that the figures to be used in drawing such a diamond are relative rather than absolute; it is the comparison with competitors' performance which counts. In addition, they are generally the result of personal judgement by the marketing strategist – and as such are as good as his 'guesses'.

 Vital questions and answers

■ The next quick exercise is – based on your own judgement – to draw a version of the diamond for your e-commerce business. What does this say about the power you have in the market?

Competitive history

Taking a more pragmatic approach, the best indicator of *future* competitive positions, in most stable markets, has been what has happened *before*. Thus, the previous reactions of competitors to a large extent determined the new competitive moves – particularly in terms of reactions to new entrants. This may come as no particular surprise to you. Instability may be created, however, if the organisations in the market differ in their structures, goals and cultures, and hence cannot easily 'read' the intentions of their competitors. Their 'inscrutability' may have helped Japanese entrants to destabilise some markets, to their eventual benefit, in the 1970s and 1980s.

One of the big problems for e-commerce, however, is that the advice to forget about the theories produced by academics and simply look at competitive history, is not so easy to apply. Regrettably in e-commerce, at least for the fore-

> ## KEY CONCEPT
> What competitors have done before is the best guide to what they will do next.

seeable future, there is no such history to rely on. This may be one of the reasons why competitive strategy has been so ill-judged by some of the initial start-ups. What, then, might be the alternatives?

 Vital questions and answers

- Looking at your competitors, in the context of their longer history in conventional markets rather than their recent entry into e-commerce, what lessons can you learn about their likely future competitive positions?

Categories of competitors

The range of competitors in a market – for e-commerce – is interesting in terms of comparison with traditional markets, at least on the basis of Michael Porter's famous theories. His category of 'potential entrants' to a market is clearly much bigger in e-commerce since, for the time being at least, almost everyone is a new entrant. Interestingly, however, 'suppliers and buyers', who – although listed by Porter – are normally not considered as competitors, may be even more significant in the context of e-commerce. The idea that the suppliers can bypass retailers and wholesalers and go direct to consumers is a very potent one. This is now called *disintermediation*, and may mean that those suppliers no longer need the middle part of the existing distribution chain. On the other hand, the opposite effect can happen, as it has for example with Amazon, where the wholesaler or retailer is able to handle a much wider range of offerings and build a position on the diverse nature of its offerings. As usual, it is horses for courses. This means that the rules in particular markets, which everyone currently works by, may be turned upside down by the move to e-commerce.

Leaders and followers

Until recently, Michael Porter's work has undoubtedly been the most influential in this area, but there are other commentators with contributions to make. Thus, some emphasise a different competitive split: that between those products

> **KEY CONCEPT**
>
> Leaders gain from expanding markets, followers from promoting (and price-cutting) their way into them.

or services which have a substantial market share (typically 40% or more) ('leaders'), and those which have minor shares, with marginal positions ('followers'). The approach each of these organisations adopts may be very different:

■ *Leaders* – in this case, the 'competitive thrust' may not necessarily be the only, or even the main, objective, since they stand to gain significantly from market expansion, and their promotional effort will often include elements directed as much to this end as against their competitors. In terms of competitive activity, it is normally expected that companies with major 'brand leaders' will concentrate their effort on advertising. This has, it seems, been the strategy of some of the major e-commerce start-ups, and is often described as 'obtaining the first-mover advantage', where these are willing to invest very heavily to be the leader. As we will see later in this chapter, in the Rule of 123, being one of the first three brands in a stable market does confer significant advantages. In e-commerce, however, the advantages are much less – partly because of the lack of significant scale advantages.

■ *Followers* – here, the whole strategy is likely to be fiercely competitive, aiming only to grab the largest share possible of the existing 'cake'. In traditional markets, their main competitive device is likely to be 'below the line' promotion and, in particular, price competition. In e-commerce, there may be many more followers and this may be the normal mode of operation for most of the market. In this case, the key may well be diversity – or at least seeming diversity. E-commerce followers will attempt to segment the market to provide a niche which only they can address.

To which of these categories do you and, in turn, your competitors belong?

■ *Know your competitors* – by far the most important aspect of effective competitive strategy is that you get to know your competitors personally!

Competitors' response

Thus, one of the aptitudes which marks great generals, as much as chess masters, is their ability to get under the skin of their opponents, to understand them in such a way that they can predict what their responses to different situations might be. So probably the most important, but often neglected, aspect of any competitor research is to determine how each of your competitors may respond to future changes. In traditional markets, there are four possible categories of response:

- *Non-response* (or slow response) – this competitor will not respond directly to any changes in the environment, or at least not in the short term. It may be a dominant brand leader, or it may be a competitor in a particularly weak position which cannot resource any reaction. Due to the relative lack of competitive advantages, this response may predominate in e-commerce markets. The participants should thank their lucky stars for this, since it lets many more players remain in the game!

> **KEY CONCEPT**
>
> Conventional competitive responses may not be needed in many e-commerce markets.

- *Focused response* – some competitors will only respond to certain types of challenge (typically on price). This is likely to be the other main response in e-commerce markets where, due to the sheer numbers involved, most participants will focus on the bits of the market close to them and on a limited number of competitors which they see as intruders to their own territory. Their behaviour may be compared to the territoriality shown by some animals.

- *Fast response* – there are also a few organisations which have a policy of immediate and substantial response (often a deliberate 'overkill') – as much to deter future challengers as to respond to the current threat. If this strategy is possible (it is really only available to leaders in the largest sectors), and can be resourced, it is usually the most effective, and the most cost-effective, since the sooner the threat is removed the sooner high profits can be generated again. It is recommended that this is your own strategy – just as long as it is practical, and you can afford it, which may only be the case for a few brands in e-commerce.

♦ *Unpredictable response* – the most difficult to deal with and the most dangerous (to themselves as much as to others), however, are those organisations whose responses cannot be predicted at all! Due to the ignorance of the managers in many new start-ups, this has often been the outcome, by default, across many of the new e-commerce markets. Even so, you should never adopt this strategy unless all else has failed.

 Vital questions and answers

■ Which of these responses do you follow?
■ Is this an effective strategy?
■ Which of these responses do your competitors follow?

One good thing about e-commerce is that existence of the Internet means that you can track every competitive move from the comfort of your desk. You can use software agents to track these, but why bother when all you need to do is to have a list of their websites in your browser? Every morning you can check what they are up to!

As a help with this process, I offer a brief checklist:

 IMPLEMENTATION CHECKLIST

■ Are you a 'leader', one of the 123?
■ If so, is your main preoccupation expanding the market (so that competing with everyone else takes second priority)?

- Or are you a follower?
- In which case, how will you fight? By price-cutting, by below-the-line marketing or by niche marketing?
- What does competitive history tell you?
- Will competitor response be slow, focused, fast or unpredictable?
- What will be your own response strategy?

Branding

As suggested earlier, branding is probably the most important marketing device for services in general and in particular for e-commerce, where so much is intangible.

The need is for something unique to hang the product offering around, and that something is usually the brand. Indeed, the epitome of differentiation in e-commerce is that of 'branding'.

> **KEY CONCEPT**
>
> Branding is especially important in e-commerce.

The product or service (including now those of non-profit organisations) is given a 'character', an 'image', almost a personality. This is based first of all on a name (the brand), but then also on the other factors affecting image which have built up over time, and which have been influenced by elements such as the packaging, advertising and, in particular in the context of e-commerce, website design. The aim is to make the brand so unique that it effectively has its own separate market. This is most often seen as the overt branding of a product or, especially in e-commerce, a service which is sold direct to customers. Recently, however, we have seen the development of what may be described as *derived* branding, where a supplier of an ingredient used by a number of suppliers to the end-user brands the ingredient itself, thus attempting to set up an brand monopoly for that ingredient.

In traditional markets, an example of this is the use of the artificial sweetener Aspartame in soft drinks. Most obviously, though, it is seen in Intel's campaign, 'Intel Inside', to ensure that its microprocessor is used in PCs. It is especially to be seen, in e-commerce, in the practice of affiliate marketing, where the branding task may often be shared. In e-commerce, Microsoft, for example, co-brands (and in effect co-promotes) parts of its website with the PC vendors who sell Windows pre-installed on their machines.

In economic terms the 'brand' can be a device for creating a 'monopoly' or at least a form of 'imperfect competition', so that the brand owner can obtain some of the benefits related to decreased price competition. Most 'branding', in this context, is established by promotional means, even if only by the website itself. But the monopoly position may also be extended, or even created, by patents and intellectual property. In all these contexts, 'own label' brands (the brands of a retailer, for example) can be just as powerful, and indeed some of these are already perceived by consumers as the 'brand leaders' in their markets.

In e-commerce, the brand becomes even more important – often all-important – since it is often the only thing that differentiates one offering from another. Without a brand, or without a clearly differentiated product or service, there is nothing on which to build a position in the marketplace.

Customer franchise

The mirror image of the brand value is often referred to as the 'customer franchise'. At one extreme it may come from the individual relationship developed face to face by the sales professional in industrial markets, and something approaching this may be achieved by one-to-one marketing in some e-commerce markets. At the other extreme, it is the cumulative image, held by the consumer, resulting from long exposure to all aspects of the product or service and especially to a number of advertising and promotional campaigns. In some markets the customer franchise may be so strong as to be exclusive, in effect giving the supplier a monopoly with those customers.

It needs to be recognised, however, that the traditional view of loyal customers never buying any other brand has been shown to be largely untrue. Thus, almost *all* consumers regularly switch brands,

> **KEY CONCEPT**
>
> Loyal customers still switch brands – but tend to favour one.

purely for variety, but they may still retain an image of their favourite brand, which will swing the balance when their next purchase decision is taken. It may thus still have a value (upon which the advertiser can build) even if their current purchasing decision goes against it. A later decision may, once again, swing in its favour. The customer franchise is, therefore, a very tangible asset in terms of its potential effect on sales, even if it is intangible in every other respect. One great advantage of (one-to-one) e-commerce, through clubs for example, is that it is very easy, and very cost-effective, to maintain 'member loyalty' even through the times when they temporarily defect to other brands.

This loyalty is based on an accumulation of impacts over time. Unfortunately, too many marketers – particularly those in creative departments within advertising agencies – signally fail to recognise the importance, and long-term nature, of this investment. They treat each new campaign as if it could, and should, be taken in isolation, no matter how it meshes with previous messages which have been delivered to the consumer. The evidence is that the consumer, however, does not view the advertising and promotion in isolation; instead she incorporates it into her existing image of the company – to good or bad effect, depending upon how well the new campaign complements the old. This may also be a problem for website developers, unless they take full advantage of the inherent flexibility to allow the individual to create their own brand.

All of this may sound very familiar, and you may be asking what happened to the brand which is said to be the major investment. You will be reassured to learn that there is no contradiction in this. The consumer franchise is, to all practical intents, the external alter ego of the brand. The brand is how the producer typically sees the (internal) investment. The customer franchise is the outcome of that internal investment; the counterbalancing entry with the customers.

Branding policies

For the record, there are a number of possible policies – that apply to e-commerce markets as well as to conventional ones – for creating such brands:

> **KEY CONCEPT**
>
> Most brands are still company names.

 GETTING STARTED

- *Company name* – often, especially in the industrial sector, it is just the company's name, or website's name (where this is different, such as is the case for the 'Egg' bank), which is promoted.

Does this apply to your organisation?

- *Family branding* – a very strong brand name (or company name) can be made the vehicle for a range of products. This process seems to have been taken furthest by P&G by connecting separate families through shared branded ingredients such as its 'Excel' cleaning ingredient. On the other hand, Unilever has deliberately launched a new brand, 'Enjoy', globally in order to cover as wide a range as possible – and will, in effect, transfer some of its existing minor brands to this stable. It is possible that portals, or even clusters of sites within these, will adopt this approach, and even Amazon now uses its name to cover a wide range of offerings, which even include 'auctions' in competition with eBay!

Does this apply to your organisation?

- *Individual branding* – this is where each brand has a separate name, which may even compete against other brands from the same company. Of course, many companies, especially new start-ups, may have a stand-alone brand. Lastminute.com has established itself with a very clear identity as a service which offers bargains on airline tickets and last-minute travel offers.

Does this apply to your organisation?

What approach would be most suitable for your organisation's e-commerce brands, and how might this be implemented?

In terms of existing products, brands may be *developed* in a number of ways:

 GETTING STARTED

- *Brand extension* – the existing strong brand name can be used as a vehicle for new or modified products. Even in traditional

> **KEY CONCEPT**
>
> Brand extension is especially important to e-commerce.

markets, this now appears to be the most prevalent form of development, which is understandable since it maximises the considerable investment in the brand name. In e-commerce markets, though, *most* of the successful brands will probably be extended from existing brands which companies are already selling. Barnes & Noble (www.barnesandnoble.com), as compared with Amazon, has high-street bookshops and this means that their brand is already established.

The effect of the extension of the brand into e-commerce is to add in another *delivery* system. This is a much less onerous 'new product launch' than is normally considered to be the case, even for a brand extension in a conventional market. In any case, brand extensions, which have tended to dominate new brand activity in such traditional markets over the past couple of decades, are almost always into a *nearby* sector. For example, Procter & Gamble's Fairy Liquid dishwashing liquid brand has been extended into a number of other related fields. Coca-Cola has, over time, launched a number of variants on Coca-Cola, even though this has just involved marketing different tastes – sometimes by accident! It is even more likely that extensions into e-commerce will also target nearby sectors – most likely they will be positioned in *exactly* the same sector as the parent organisation already trades in! The risks involved will therefore be much lower than for start-ups, so many of which have failed in recent years.

In e-commerce, the extension is quite simply to a different *place*. Taking the parallel example of Coca-Cola in conventional markets, the biggest difference it faces is often simply between Coca-Cola sold in a supermarket or over the counter in a restaurant or bar – but not, as it happens, over the Internet. Accordingly, the extension of a brand into e-commerce, for a strong existing brand, is a relatively simple matter – and it is for this reason that extensions of existing brands are likely to prove the most successful, at least in the short term. The Rule of 123 says that investment in the brand leader, and the three top brands, will keep almost everyone else out. Taken from the other direction, this also says the first entrants into a market have the first-mover advantage, but that is only true for an e-commerce market where there are no equivalents of established brands in conventional markets.

- *Multibrands* – alternatively, in a market that is fragmented amongst a number of brands, a supplier can choose to launch totally new brands in apparent competition with its own existing strong brand(s). This may happen in e-commerce, where an offering (or a set of offerings) is branded separately (and probably under different website addresses) to different audiences. Some of the most interesting developments in e-commerce may follow this pattern, with products competing – probably on different promotional platforms – with their parent's other brands in conventional markets as well as e-commerce. So far this has most clearly been seen in the financial sector with, for example, Egg following a very different strategy to its parent, the Prudential bank.

Whatever the distribution method, e-commerce or otherwise, branding has traditionally been seen as almost exclusively the territory of consumer goods companies, but it has much wider application than that. *All* organisations, whether they sell to consumers or industrial users, whether they offer products or services, whether they are profit-making or non-profit making, have at least one brand, which is usually the name of the organisation. This may come as a surprise, or even as a shock, to those organisations who focus on the product or service they produce, and who think brands are only for goods which appear on supermarket shelves. Nothing could be further from the truth.

The brand encapsulates the product/service package. This package is usually very complex, and almost always contains a range of intangibles in addition to the physical elements – indeed in e-commerce it may be almost totally made up of such intangible elements. As a result, it has to have some form of symbolic representation, a tangible peg on which to hang all these other elements. Sometimes that may be a symbol or logo, on the design of which some organisations (including government departments) spend a small fortune and which is meant to symbolise the character of the brand. In the case of many of the new start-ups in e-commerce markets it is also the web address (such as Lastminute.com). More generally, and often just as effectively, it is simply the name of the product or service, or – most often of all – that of the organisation.

Many people would argue that the (brand) name in itself is critical. Certainly, when you are launching a brand name it helps considerably if the name describes the 'product' in some way or other. International Business Machines very clearly described what the company was about, as did Alka Seltzer. But most suitable names have long since been claimed and these days you are likely to be limited to neutral names which are at best inoffensive (often now deliberately selected to be usable around the world – Kodak, Exxon etc.), which is an important point – the owners of the very successful 'Sweat' soft drink brand in Japan may have difficulty in bringing it to the West! This, no doubt, was the justification for some of the dot.com brands. It clearly was true of the name 'Lastminute.com', which does sum up its offering, of last-minute travel bargains, and also indicates that it is a website-based company. It even manages to give its web address: all of this in one word! It is less obvious how 'Boo.com' indicated what its business might be – a problem which afflicted many other similar start-ups who were so busy trying to get a memorable address across that they didn't seem to worry too much about what it said about the company!

On the other hand, it is what you manage to associate – over time – with that brand name which represents the real strength of the brand. IBM, as it is now called, is meaningless as an English word, yet it resonates with very powerful associations, and this is just as true of McDonalds – and I don't even have to say what the product here is, since the brand is so powerful that there can only be one possibility! Coca-Cola, perhaps the most powerful brand of all, would have very negative connotations if its buyers took its name seriously and associated it with the drug which was essential to its original medical properties, but which has long since been dropped from its formulation.

The most powerful brands encapsulate a bewildering array of elements, even those in e-commerce markets, so it is best to think of them in almost human terms – as if they had the complex physical characteristics and personality of one of your friends. It may often be just as true of the way that the consumers think about the brand: their favourites are their friends, they're the ones they feel comfortable with, the ones they can take home knowing they will fit in with their lifestyle. If you can think how they could be changed to become better friends to the consumers – much as you would change to fit in with your circle of friends, by wearing suitable clothes, talking about the things which interest them, doing the same things together – then you are on your way to developing a successful brand. This is just as true of the weightiest of brands, such as those in capital goods (like IBM) or medicine. The personality they need to establish may be a professional one (like a doctor or engineer, say) but the same rules still apply.

Perhaps the most important fact, and one which is sadly neglected in most organisations, is that the brand is the most important and valuable investment owned by any organisation, even in e-commerce where – in the absence of physical assets – it should often be seen as even more important. It contains all the value which has

been added to the organisation by its investments in service to the customer over the years: image, reputation, loyalty, trust, etc. These assets are normally worth far more than the stocks and equipment which feature on most balance sheets. On the few occasions when a brand valuation actually has been added to the balance sheet it has dwarfed everything else, as during the Nestlé takeover of Rowntree.

 Vital questions and answers

- Which approach does your organisation mainly use – brand extension or multibrand?
- What might you estimate the value of your organisation's brand(s) to be? £ . . . . million/ billion

The rule of 123

The power of the brand is seen especially with brand leaders: those in the top three slots, especially the brand leader. In FMCG markets, for instance, the brand leader often holds

40% or more of the overall market. This level is usually highly profitable, since in addition to the high value of sales generated, its strong position in the market normally allows the setting of a higher price (and hence significantly higher

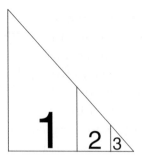

Figure 5.9: The 123 Rule

profit) and economies of scale are possible (not least in terms of promotional and distribution costs). The three leading brands, which typically dominate such markets, between them will usually hold around 70% of total sales.

The profitability that a brand leader commands usually offers, therefore, ample justification, especially over the longer term (where such brands can easily maintain leadership for decades) for the high levels of investment which are needed to achieve this position. The Japanese corporations who were willing to make such long-term investments in markets during the 1970s and 1980s have since been extremely well rewarded for their efforts.

The rule is that, in a stable market, the brand leader should hold twice the share of the second company and three times that of the third. Figure 5.9 illustrates this concept.

The exact ratios vary from market to market, and even the average may vary, depending upon which parcel of products is examined. The Boston Consulting Group,[10] for example, also suggest that the brand leader should hold twice the share of the second brand, but they suggest that it should hold four times that of the third brand (giving a rule of 1:2:4). But, at

---

[10] Henderson, B.D. (1985) *The Rule of Three and Four*, Boston, Boston Consulting Group.

least in traditional consumer markets, the general principle of the 123 Rule seems to hold. With such diversity appearing in e-commerce markets, it is not yet clear whether anything like this rule will appear there but, until the position is clear, the safest bet is that this rule should also apply to larger e-commerce markets too.

 Vital questions and answers

- What is the market position (1st, 2nd, 3rd etc.) of your leading brand(s)?
- Does it (Do they) gain any benefit from the Rule of 123?
- How does this affect your marketing strategy?

Product/service decisions

CHAPTER 6

Overview

This topic has been the subject of many chapters in traditional marketing textbooks, my own books included. But where we assume that, in the case of your own organisation, this 'product' already exists in at least one conventional market and is incrementally entering the e-commerce sector, I will not repeat a great deal of that material here. To provide some historical context, however, it should be remembered that, in the cost-cutting 1990s, one popular approach – based on aggressive competition, and very effectively promoted by Michael Porter – was that of the 'value chain'.

In the context of e-commerce, the objective of this chapter is therefore to understand the new value chains, along with their economies of scale and the resulting competitive forces which are now emerging. In contrast, it directly examines the failure of the Product Life Cycle (PLC) to help in the new environment and in managing change, and its resulting replacement by devices such as the Competitive Saw and, more basically, by the 80:20 Rule. The chapter also explores how new product development may be managed in this new environment.

CONTINUED . . . Overview

- Value chains
- Sensitivity analyses
- Product life cycle (PLC)
- Competitive saw
- 80:20 (Pareto) rule
- New products
- Creative imitation

Value chains

Michael Porter[11] divided the elements of his value chain into nine parts:

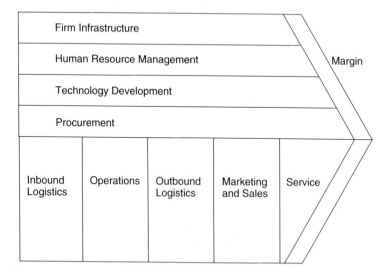

Figure 6.1: Michael Porter's value chain

---

[11] Porter, M. (1985) *Competitive Advantage*, New York, Free Press.

In theory, each of these elements is to be investigated separately, to optimise the value it adds to the product/service, but he also suggests you look at the links between them.

Although he carefully stresses that the investigation should look at added value in terms of 'differentiation' (his word for those activities which improve the customer's perceived value of the product or service by making it seem different to its competitors) as much as in terms of reduced costs, it is the latter aspect (of 'cost reduction') which tends to dominate his work – and that of many of his followers. In theory, at least, this concept should be just as applicable to e-commerce. The reality was, however, that even for traditional markets most of these elements were much harder to cost than Porter allowed for. In many of them, 'allocation of overheads' was the main determinant of the booked cost – and was clearly a matter of (suspect) judgement rather than of record! In the even more intangible fields covered by e-commerce it may be almost impossible to get hard costs for most elements. The result is that managers tend to focus on those few areas where they *can* cut costs, regardless of whether this will be productive or not.

Sensitivity analysis

The focus on costs can, however, still be illuminating if handled properly.

Thus, one especially enlightening approach is to take the cost(s) in each of the areas (or part of an area) separately, and see what happens (in percentage terms) to the overall margin when each of these individual costs is reduced by 10%. Reductions in some areas will have little impact on the overall margin (and hence can be safely treated as of lower priority in a cost reduction exercise). Some areas,

> **KEY CONCEPT**
>
> Sensitivity analysis can be used to prioritise product strategy.

though, will produce significant changes in the overall margin; these are the ones to which the margin is said to be most sensitive, and attention should be focused on these. In this way, determining the elements which have the greatest (percentage) impact on the overall organisation is a powerful device for focusing attention on key cost issues. This approach is just as powerful for e-commerce and may well be one of few options open to planners in this sector.

One other benefit of the value chain approach is that it highlights aspects of the chain which are critical to the organisation's work. For example, this form of analysis often shows – in traditional markets – that distribution (in its most general sense) is much more important than managers think. In e-commerce such 'supporting' factors may become the heart of the new business.

Practical value chains

A more practical approach is to split the activities of the organisation into those characteristic groupings which are natural to its specific operations – rather than the theoretical nine categories described by Michael Porter. In addition, his upper set of cross-organisation activities should be ignored, since – in our experience – they create problems when allocating overheads, and tend to confuse managers trying to use the approach.

If we look at the result for a typical e-commerce operation it seems very different to Michael Porter's example, but this may also be due to the different pattern of business, with purchasing of 'components' often coming *after* the sale to the consumer!

Figure 6.2 shows the visual presentation. It can be made more meaningful if the size of each segment reflects its importance (on whatever basis – volume, added value, sensitivity etc. – you decide is most useful).

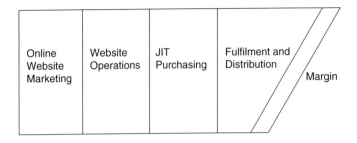

Figure 6.2: Segments in the value chain

 Vital questions and answers

- As you might expect, the exercise here is to draw a comparable diagram for your own e-commerce operations. What does this indicate about the relative priorities you should assign to each?

Product life cycle?

One other famous piece of marketing theory revolves around the *product life cycle* (PLC). The life cycle has long been a very important element of (academic) marketing theory.

You should be aware, however, that its supposed universal applicability is largely a myth.[12] On the other hand, it is an important one in theory, which you will need to appreciate before you can dismiss it!

> **KEY CONCEPT**
>
> The PLC has little practical value, especially in e-commerce.

Its 'intuitive appeal' is based on the analogy of natural (human) lives. It, thus, suggests that any product or service moves

---

[12] Mercer, D.A. (1993) A two-decade test of product life cycle theory. *British Journal of Management* **4**, 269–274.

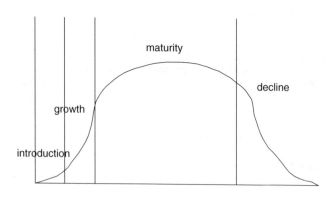

Figure 6.3: Stages in a product's life cycle

through identifiable stages, each of which is related to the passage of time (as the product or service grows older) and each of which has different characteristics (see Figure 6.3).

Lessons of the life cycle

It is true that every product or service must, almost by definition, have a life cycle. It is launched, it grows, then it dies. As such, it offers a useful model to keep at the back of your mind. If you are in the introductory or growth phases, as many e-commerce operations are, or in a phase of decline (which some of the original start-ups have already moved to!), perhaps it should be at the front of your mind, for the predominant features of these phases may be those revolving around such organisational life and death. Between these two extremes, it is salutary to have that vision of mortality in front of you.

The most important aspect of product life cycles is, however, that to all practical intents and purposes they often do not exist, even in traditional markets. In most of

KEY CONCEPT

In the context of the brand manager's typical three-year plan, brand life cycles do not exist.

these markets the majority of the major (dominant) brands have held their position for at least two decades. The dominant product life cycle is therefore one of continuity! The same may also apply to existing brands being extended into e-commerce markets – it is their overall life cycle, across all markets, which matters. At the other end of the scale, the dynamics of 'pure' e-commerce markets merely add to the problems for PLC enthusiasts. Life cycles in e-commerce markets are so fast that there is not time for a 'natural' life cycle to become established, before the product dies an unnatural death.

In the most respected criticism of the product life cycle, Dhalla and Yuspeh[13] state:

> . . . clearly, the PLC is a dependent variable which is determined by market actions; it is not an independent variable to which companies should adapt their marketing programs. Marketing management itself can alter the shape and duration of a brand's life cycle.

Thus, the life cycle may sometimes be useful as a description of conventional markets, but not as a predictor; and usually should be firmly under the control of the marketer! The important point is that in many, if not most, traditional markets the product or brand life cycle is significantly *longer* than the planning cycle of the organisations involved. In e-commerce, on the other hand, it is too *short* for planners to use. It, thus, offers little of practical value for most marketers in either case. Even if the PLC exists for them, their plans will be based simply upon that piece of the curve where they currently reside (probably in the 'mature' stage for conventional markets – including extensions into e-commerce – and the introductory phase for

---

[13] Dhalla, N.K. and Yuspeh, S. (1976) Forget the product life cycle concept. *Harvard Business Review*, January–February.

'pure' e-commerce). In the former, the planners' view of that part of it will almost certainly be linear, and will not encompass the whole range from growth to decline. In the latter case, it will be even narrower – and more unpredictable. Its sensitivity to the exact 'starting point' means that it most closely follows the mathematics of chaos theory!

Whatever the underlying reason for its failure, the use of the PLC may not be just a waste of time but can be positively dangerous for many organisations. At one extreme it tempts managers of successful, mature brands to prematurely anticipate their move into decline. At the other, the exciting newness of the activities on the Internet may seduce them into ignoring the needs of the main (conventional) brand. But it is probably the most widely known, taught and respected piece of marketing theory! It is imperative, therefore, that – before using it or even dismissing it – you appreciate the *problems* that its use, in any form, might pose.

How might you manage change?

It would be useful to have some theory which explains the likely outcomes over time. Thus, in the longer term, seeing in advance the fractures in the environment which might threaten survival or even recognising their implications after they have occurred, is very difficult. This is best handled by environmental analysis, 'scanning', which is part of long range planning. It requires you to take input from a wide range of sources – typically the media – to see which unexpected changes in society are likely to impact your business. The end point of such a process is often scenario forecasting, which is becoming increasingly important.[14]

[14] Mercer, D. (1998) *Marketing Strategy: The challenge of the external environment*, London, Sage.

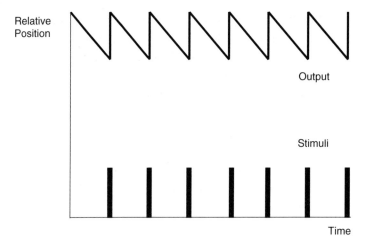

Figure 6.4: The competitive saw

Responding to situations once they have been detected is perhaps best ensured by undertaking the most effective possible marketing – better than that of other organisations which might also attempt to take advantage of the change – and, most important of all, reacting much faster than these competitors.

The less dramatic changes which regularly occur in a stable market – and even in a rapidly growing one – are the staple diet of most marketers. These are dealt with especially poorly by the PLC. The technique which has accordingly been developed, as a positive alternative to the ineffective use of the PLC in this (mature) range, is called the *competitive saw*, and is shown in Figure 6.4.

The principles involved are very simple, as is indicated by Figure 6.4.

1 Every *stimulus* (every investment, whether it is an advertising or promotional campaign or a new feature added to a website) results, after a short delay, in a rapid improvement in *output*, raising the product or service's

position (typically directly in terms of its competitive position, and indirectly in terms of sales levels).

2   This advantage is then steadily *diluted* as competitors invest in their own activities, upgrading their own web pages for instance, and the performance level (the competitive advantage or actual sales) slowly drops until the next stimulus is applied. Because of the competitive aspect and because it largely removes variations due to seasonality etc., the measurements are usually in terms of relative share (though absolute figures may also be used).

This is a very simplified model of what actually happens, although something approaching it can be observed in practice (in the way that, for instance, advertising agencies routinely track the impact of advertising campaigns on awareness levels or website owners similarly track their hit levels), which is not the case with the product life cycle which it replaces. Despite its simplicity, it offers a number of significant benefits:

- *Intimations of mortality* – it effectively replaces the one important function of the product life cycle, that of reminding managers that there will be no future if they do not look after their brands or ignore them to concentrate on e-commerce – but it does this more directly and practically, and without the major drawbacks inherent in the PLC model.
- *Timescaling* – on much the same theme, it is an ever-present reminder that you cannot neglect your brands, or stop investing in them, for too long – especially during the extended 'maturity' phase of a successful brand.
- *Linkage of inputs and outputs* – it encourages, and provides a framework for, managers to actively plan what inputs are

needed, when, and what the outputs will be; and what the efficiency of conversion of inputs to outputs is. This is especially important during the start-up period of an e-commerce operation, when little else may be known.

• *Surfacing of investment* – it makes very clear the need for, and the results of, investment policies on brands – in e-commerce or otherwise.

Thus, the three main lessons of the competitive saw are the importance of relative performance, the time-related nature of this, and the investments which lie underneath.

Adopting the long-term perspective implied by the last of these observations reveals another important implication. Following the implied principle of a fixed asset, on to this shorter-term sawtooth maintenance pattern can be overlaid a gradually declining trend in performance, equivalent to *depreciation* in financial accounting. Over time there may be a slow drift away from the ideal position, as the customers' needs and wants change and/or competitive positioning improves.

Your own response to this may take two forms:

 GETTING STARTED

1 Perhaps the most effective response is *dynamic repositioning*. The need for change is regularly tracked and the brand's position readjusted, in much the same way that an autopilot's feedback mechanisms ensure that an airliner follows the correct flight path. The emphasis here is on the dynamic approach to (current) change, where most of marketing theory

> **KEY CONCEPT**
>
> 'Dynamic repositioning' and 'brand depreciation' are needed to protect the brand investment.

revolves around decisions based upon static (historic) positions. Clearly, in a dynamic environment such as that of e-commerce, this is essential.

2 If such dynamic repositioning is not possible, perhaps because the necessary product changes come in discrete steps, then periodic readjustments may be needed. This is where the concept of *depreciation* is especially valuable. It allows the build-up of reserves to cover the significant costs of such repositioning exercises. This is one investment many e-commerce start-ups have, to their cost, ignored!

The investment in a successful brand needs to be maintained both in the short term, by regular marketing programmes funded from annual budgets, and in the longer term, by less frequent major investments (in repositioning and relaunching) which require reserves provided by a depreciation fund.

Encouraged by PLC theory, which seems to emphasise the futility of long-term investment, the long-term asset investment aspect of brand performance is often ignored by traditional marketing theory. This is compounded, in the e-commerce sector, by the sheer excitement of living from day to day, when any long-term effects – even those just months away – seem too remote to consider. We believe that, on the contrary, investment for the longer term should represent the main element of marketing strategy and (in view of the danger it poses for the unwary) the short-term messages given by the PLC should be dropped.

Vital questions and answers

■ Does your organisation employ dynamic repositioning as a matter of policy?

CONTINUED ... Vital questions and answers

- Should it?
- If it did so, what would be the impact on its e-commerce operations? And what would be the impact of it applying brand depreciation?

The 80:20 rule and ABC analysis

On the other hand, the most general and most powerful rule of all – including in e-commerce – is the 80:20 rule. It states that, across a wide range of situations, 20% of the contributors (products or services, say) will account for 80% of the performance (volume of sales, say). The 80:20 rule has been in use for more than a century. First postulated by an Italian, Pareto (hence its alternative title, the Pareto rule), it is just as relevant today. It is still a very productive tool, and one of the few general ones which can be applied to almost any marketing situation.

It recognises that an organisation's distribution of potential, in terms of products or customers, will almost inevitably be skewed. Some of these will be more important than others (and some

> **KEY CONCEPT**
>
> The 80:20 rule is especially valuable in the e-commerce environment.

much more important). That the typical skew is so large that 80% of sales, say, come from 20% of customers (and conversely that 80% of customers contribute no more than 20% of turnover) may come as a surprise, but this has been borne out by countless practical examples. However, as it is only a general principle and not an exact equation, the outcome may be 70:30 or 90:10 (but, by definition, it will almost never be 50:50).

Its power comes from the fact that it enables you to concentrate your resources on just 20% of activities, confident that these are the important ones, responsible for 80% of your business. You can then safely limit any investment in the other 80%. This is especially productive when deciding the priorities for your website, or the systems associated with it. The first decision must be which 20% will have the greatest impact!

One especially useful way to take advantage of this is when you are listing the results of any analysis. Simply print the output in descending order of importance – by descending order of sales volumes, for instance. In this way, the key items are always at the top and receive your immediate attention. On the other hand, the minor ones are at the bottom where it does not matter if they are ignored. This may sound trivial, but it may revolutionise your view of the world. No longer will those customers, and products, whose name starts with the letter 'A' dominate your life!

 Vital questions and answers

- Take some of the reports you regularly use, such as those on product/service revenues or customer income, and reorganise (ie sort) them in descending order of performance. How does this affect your perception of what they say?

New products

Moving on to another part of the traditional marketing mix, the current best guess is that the most important – or the most *radical* – new products will eventually appear in the Customer-to-Customer C2C) arena. As with most new products, and certainly with the most radical new products, it may not yet be obvious what they are. More important, perhaps, it is not even possible to research them with consumers, because they have even less of an idea about them than the suppliers.

Having said that, much of the 'new product' work, like that in traditional markets, will be about *incremental* developments. These are much easier to predict, and certainly much easier to manage. On the other hand, the

> **KEY CONCEPT**
>
> Most 'new products' emerge from incremental developments.

voracious nature of e-commerce means that many more of them will be needed and the result may be that there will be a switch from the Western model, of small numbers of carefully researched new products, to the Japanese model, where large numbers of products and services are launched simultaneously and are allowed to 'churn' in the marketplace. The decision is in effect then left to the consumers in the marketplace. Those products which survive are the ones which the suppliers then back. This was a dubious model where massive investment was required in conventional markets, because significant investment was still required to ensure that the distribution channel got behind the product. With e-commerce and the Internet such investments are very much less costly. Accordingly, we should expect to see far more churning of new products, with them being dumped on to the marketplace and the attrition rate being sorted out there rather than in laboratories or the marketing teams' offices.

The customer bonus

In terms of new products, especially in e-commerce, the best R&D of all is to let the customer or consumer tell you how the product or service should be developed. This approach is most obvious in those industrial

> **KEY CONCEPT**
>
> Customers are a valuable source of new product developments/ideas.

markets where some customers naturally undertake a substantial share of application development: that is, the work on the uses to which the product or service will be put. Observing this is especially easy to undertake in e-commerce markets (B2B as well as B2C) where interaction with these customers can be almost continuous. Sound development strategy in these cases may therefore simply be based upon observing what these customers are doing, and selecting the best solution(s) that emerge – and then translating them to the wider customer set. In the process, the required changes to the product or service itself may also emerge – inherent in the demands posed by these new applications.

As suggested above, the same principle can also be successfully applied to consumer products; after all, that is what much of marketing research aims to achieve. On the other hand, as for example practised by the Japanese, it can be approached more simply and directly and hence much better, intuitively understood by the manager. Often multiple versions of the product or service are launched for the ultimate test of consumer taste – those which sell best represent the customers voting with their wallets. On the other hand, they are fortunate (or wise) in having a Japanese public educated to try the many new products brought to market. However, though traditional markets may be more conservative, much the same might now also be true for e-commerce markets in the West. Certainly, it is much easier to float new offerings in this environment – though few players have adopted the Japanese approach to date.

Vital questions and answers

■ What new product developments has your organis-ation picked up from customer usage, or from ideas submitted by them?

Creative imitation

Even in e-commerce, the greatest innovation threat usually
comes from known competitors. It is important, therefore, to
monitor their developments very closely – which it is very
easy to do in this environment (where their websites are just
as open to you as to anyone else!) and to respond in kind
immediately.

Any major new change a competitor introduces must be taken seriously and immediately evaluated to
see if it is a genuine threat to (the
position of) your brand. At the same
time, where time is of the essence,
contingency plans must be prepared (and development work
on a response begun). The main point to remember is that a
brand/market leader with a strong position rarely loses that
position even to a serious threat – just so long as it delivers
an effective counter (usually by imitation) fast enough. This
should be just as true of e-commerce, but (with so many
competitors across the globe, any one of which may have
developed a killer application) it may now be difficult to track
all of them!

> **KEY CONCEPT**
>
> Competitors can be a
> source of creative
> developments.

Creative imitation, though, can offer wider benefits. Many
ideas can be productively transferred from other fields of
human activity. Indeed, the major technique for finding major
new product developments is scanning the horizon – known
as 'creative scanning' – preferably a decade or more ahead
(since such major developments take time as well as money).
It is true to say that the seeds of major innovations can
usually be seen a number of years (or even decades) ahead.
This is just as true of e-commerce – the technologies of the
next decade and beyond are already open to inspection,
though which ones we (or perhaps Microsoft) will choose to
exploit is much less obvious! The scientific breakthroughs

which lead to new technologies normally follow this rule, but so also do the changes in lifestyles which lead to new consumer demands.

Vital questions and answers

- What new product developments have been stimulated by competitors' advances?

A more sophisticated version of creative imitation is not simply to launch an imitation (although this may also be done to protect the immediate market position) but to put a very high level of resources into developing the next generation of products based on the imitation, and launching this *before* the competitor; thus leapfrogging it. This is especially suitable for use in e-commerce, where such product generation is rapid, and where the costs of the technological investments are relatively low.

The Japanese have managed to turn this almost into an art form, by their mastery of time management in the field of product development. In part this comes from the practices which they have built up in their manufacturing systems which stress time (JIT, for example) as much as flexibility. What is not appreciated, however, is that these are not production techniques in the Western sense, but are an outcome of many years of training their workforce to apply such approaches. Despite some 'experts' who promise to instantaneously provide you with the secrets of the Japanese, you would be wise to assume that

> **KEY CONCEPT**
>
> Leapfrogging development to the next generation, running in parallel with current development, is especially important for e-commerce.

they take decades to become effective (as they did at Toyota), rather than a matter of days.

In the area of product development, however, the Japanese use another technique – *parallel development*. Western organisations complete one stage of development before they start the next, because they believe, quite correctly, that otherwise development effort may be wasted (as each stage sets unexpected requirements for the next). The Japanese recognise this inefficiency, but believe that the benefit gained from parallel development, which is a much faster overall development process (with overlap of stages giving still faster times, despite some of the work having to be redone), far outweighs the extra costs, since it gives them market leadership. It should also be noted, however, that recently some Japanese corporations (Toyota among them) have been reducing the amount of parallel work they do because – in traditional markets – it has become too expensive. Where e-commerce markets involve much lower levels of invest-ment, however, it may still be a sound strategy – though few organisations currently seem to be considering anything as sophisticated as this!

 Vital questions and answers

■ What impact might parallel development have on your new product strategies?

Existing market leaders may take this process a stage further, by having *two* development teams working in parallel. While one is implementing the last stages of the next generation, the other is working on the earlier stages of the next generation but one, as shown in Figure 6.5.

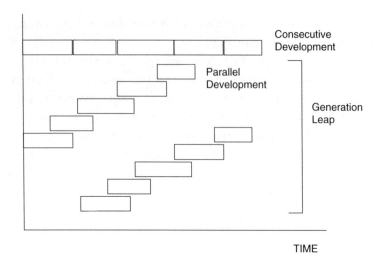

TIME

 Figure 6.5: Two teams working on parallel development

Vital questions and answers

■ How does your own organisation approach its new product development, especially in the context of e-commerce?

■ Does it track customer developments, to gain the 'customer bonus'?

■ Does it track competitive developments, to employ 'creative imitation'?

Diffusion of innovation

The theory outlined above should be directly applicable to e-commerce. But as yet it is difficult to establish the balance of the various elements, the technology distribution pattern versus that of the existing product category. It is still too early to say which diffusion patterns have built up and if they are actually any different to existing ones. At the moment it looks very much like the existing diffusion patterns, with the consumer's peers – on the same level rather than trickling down from higher levels – leading the pack. On the other hand, it may be that one can more clearly identify those product and peer group leaders, and because of the direct nature of the Internet it may be possible to motivate them more directly. But as yet no one – not even Amazon – seems to have managed to achieve this!

Pricing or promotion?

CHAPTER 7

Overview

This chapter completes the trio of chapters examining the marketing mix, by looking at those main elements outside of the product or service itself. It starts by looking at the factor which most economists, and not a few marketing theorists, focus on: price. The aim of this section is to put pricing theory in perspective as one (albeit important) element of the marketing mix and then to suggest how it might be handled in practice.

The second section moves on to another of the original 4Ps, that of *promotion*, looking at it in the pragmatic context of the consumer expectations against actual performance which is especially important in e-commerce. Finally, starting with the economies of scale argument which underpins much of pricing theory, this chapter examines the competitive forces likely to emerge in e-commerce.

- Pricing theory
- Pricing roulette in practice
- Price premium

CONTINUED . . . Overview

- Historical pricing
- Competitive pricing
- New product prices
- Advertising believability
- Complaint handling
- Dissatisfaction

Pricing

The pricing model adopted by e-commerce vendors seems, so far, to emphasise commodity prices; in other words, low prices dominate the markets. In view of the one-to-one nature of e-commerce this is a surprising, indeed perverse, effect. Instead it should be argued that, by matching the product to the exact customer, there should be an overwhelming argument for premium prices. Thus, the price wars that have emerged are unnecessary.

Thus, as an antidote to the hype which has traditionally surrounded it, let us look at some of the history of pricing theory.

Its exaggerated importance may be seen to descend from the tradition set by the economic disciplines. Central to the writings of neoclassical economists are the laws of supply and demand, which describe one theory of how prices are set.

> **KEY CONCEPT**
>
> Economic theory stresses the importance of price above all else.

Here, the price is set when the market 'clears': a technical term for a very simple principle – this happens when the price is as attractive to buyers as it is to sellers, and all the goods offered for sale are actually sold.

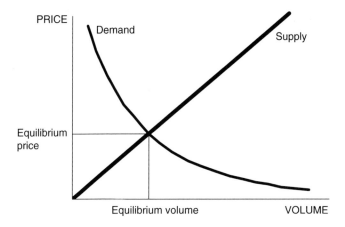

Figure 7.1: Supply and demand, and price-setting

But the typical *demand* curve of most products or services is much steeper than traditionally assumed. In essence the demand is relatively inelastic (with respect to price). At the same time the *supply* curve is very elastic above the entry price (the price

> **KEY CONCEPT**
>
> In economic theory, the price is set where the demand graph crosses that of supply.

at which the market becomes attractive to new entrants). The problem is that even a model which has been modified to take account of this will still describe price activity in only one context – that where price counts, and 'commodity' prices obtain. As we will see below, this is not normally the case.

On the other hand, when the operators within a market do decide that their products or services should be treated as commodities, and be priced accordingly, then something like the traditional picture holds. Fortunately, this applies to only a small minority of markets, and – as we have seen above – most e-commerce markets (with their matching of individual requirements) should not fall into this category.

Pricing roulette

1 The first, and most important, decision for any manager in pricing his or her product/service package is the simple one: 'Is it in a market which is based on commodity prices?' If the products or services are treated as commodities, and if prices reflect this, then you *must* do the same in order to survive, even in the short term.

2 Conversely, if the market is not commodity-based, you *must* adopt price maximisation rules. *Pricing is either commodity-based or not*: for once, there is no half-way house! This applies equally to e-commerce markets, where – with fixed price lists on public view – the evidence needed to answer this question may be much easier to find.

Much the same as you play Russian roulette with a revolver, suppliers often play pricing roulette with the market. The odds are a little bit better – our research indicates that only a tenth of markets indulge in commodity pricing. The end effect may be much the same, however, if your spin of the chamber lands you on a commodity-based market – it is often tantamount to commercial suicide!

If the products or services are treated as commodities, and if prices reflect this, then you *must* do the same in order to survive, even in the short term. You have no pricing choice. At present this is especially true in e-commerce markets, where the customer is only a click or so away from the price being set by your competitors. You must then hope that the situation changes at some time in the future, when you can make a reasonable profit, but in the short term you can only reduce costs to staunch the bleeding.

Fortunately, as mentioned above, 90% of markets are not commodity-based, and should not even be so in e-commerce. If you come into this category you can heave a sigh of relief that you have survived the test and get on with the real marketing described in the rest of this book. If, as is usually the case in a stable market (which, unfortunately, not all e-commerce is yet), the market is not commodity-based, you should adopt price maximisation rules.

This is one of the very few situations in marketing where there are no grey areas, no spectrum of options. Beware though! One of the great temptations in marketing to which many (not least too many naïve e-commerce vendors) succumb, is to think that a significantly lower price will improve your position. *The odds show (9:1, as we saw above) that this is likely to be a mistake* – and may switch the whole market to commodity pricing (so that everyone loses, especially the initiator). The good news is that there is, fortunately, little evidence that the most debilitating sort of price wars have yet broken out in e-commerce. There is, though, plenty of evidence of margins being hit by vendors selling below the optimum price.

This is not to say that a drive for reduced *costs*, which is typically initiated by commodity pricing, should be abandoned. There should always be an awareness that commodity pricing may one day emerge into your market, even if this would be near suicidal for all involved. The organisation has (while making its investments in the future), therefore, to develop a cost structure which will enable it to survive even this eventuality – and in the meantime it will reap even higher levels of profit.

 Vital questions and answers

- Now for the easiest question in this whole book: is pricing in the market(s) in which your organisation operates *commodity* or *premium* based?
- Has your organisation asked itself this question, and has it got the answer right?

Price premium

The most profitable result should be that, in the great majority of markets including those of e-commerce, suppliers can, happily for them, count on achieving more than the base commodity price.

The difference is known as the price premium which simply states that you can achieve a premium price above the commodity price level, as shown in Figure 7.2.

> **KEY CONCEPT**
>
> Achieving a price premium is the most profitable policy.

This is a simple concept, but a useful one – not least because it acts as an antidote to the temptation to indulge in price-cutting. This figure also indicates that, in most traditional markets (though not necessarily to the same extent in e-commerce markets), the brand leaders are progressively placed to achieve such premiums (though they may choose to trade this off against higher volumes of sales).

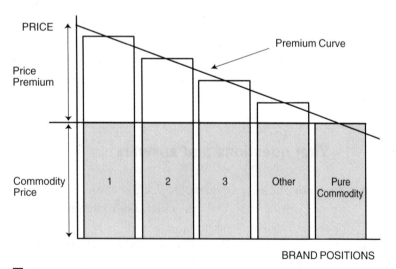

Figure 7.2: The price premium concept

The premium may be justified by a variety of factors, including those of image, quality, differentiation positioning, etc. The exact reason for the premium is not important, since it will vary from situation to situation. What is crucial is that you recognise it as a possibility, *and work to maximise it.*

If you avoid the pitfall of commodity-pricing, along with that of the many 'guaranteed' techniques of pricing offered by academics and consultants, most pricing – in conventional markets at least – then

> **KEY CONCEPT**
>
> What has happened before is the best guide to future prices.

turns out to be relatively simple. This is because most products or services are either existing products with a known track record, or are new products entering markets where there are already similar products with known track records. This, therefore, signposts the two main alternative methods, both of which tend to be scorned by academics, but which (despite the shortcomings I will discuss below) are eminently sensible.

Historical pricing

For good reasons, what the price has been in the past is, for most traditional products or services, the best starting point for what it should be in the future. Accordingly, this is probably the most prevalent form of pricing in conventional markets. On the other hand, for the obvious reason that there is rarely any significant history of pricing actions, this approach is only available in a few new sectors of 'pure' e-commerce, though it still should apply in those which are extensions of existing markets, such as the travel agency market targeted by Lastminute.com.

The first caveat is, in any case, that *you must still be aware of how the price needs to change* to reflect the consumer's changing needs and different competitive conditions – but most managers who are in touch with their customers and markets should already be well aware of such trends.

The second caveat is that *it assumes the historical price was correct*, and exactly matched the perceived value; the value which the consumer believes (perceives) the product or service holds (and hence what he is willing to pay for it). This is, though, just what the positioning process – described earlier – sets out to achieve. Pricing is just one of the variables involved in the positioning, but the process should be no less powerful for that (and, indeed, linking it to the other parameters should increase the validity of the decision). Depending upon the exact circumstances, it may even be possible to suggest that the higher levels of service (and the wider ranges offered) might justify an even higher price in some e-commerce sectors.

> ## KEY CONCEPT
>
> Pricing must allow for competitive responses.

Competitive pricing

The one additional aspect which may modify historical pricing and may sometimes replace it (and always will in the case of new products) is what competitors are doing. The positioning exercise, of course, takes full account of the relative position with respect to competitors – so, once again, this should be a natural part of the pricing process. For the obvious reason that this is often the only pricing information available in most 'pure' e-commerce markets, this is as yet the main approach adopted in practice.

Cost-plus pricing

The remaining main approach, *cost-plus pricing* which means adding a fixed percentage (to show a 'profit') to costs, should *not* usually be considered. Costs should be minimised, but prices should be maximised, based upon what the customer is willing to pay – which is typically not directly linked to cost.

The one exception, where cost-plus pricing may be justified, is that where a large number of items have to be priced – such as by Amazon – and the logistics of making a large number of individual decisions becomes a significant factor. Here a guide price may have to be determined (on the basis of historical/competitive/perceived value pricing) for a group of products, and then extended to the individual products as a percentage uplift on their cost.

***

 Vital questions and answers

■ Which approach does your organisation use (either deliberately or by default): historical/competitive/ cost-plus/other?

Pricing new products

The time when an organisation is most free to determine the price of its products or services is when they are launched. On the other hand, once the price has been set, so has a precedent. In the case of any future changes the consumers will have not only the competitive prices as a comparison, but they will also have your previous prices as a direct reference point! This makes it very difficult to make substantial changes to the prices of existing products or services. Consumer reactions may be severe if they think they are being taken advantage of. This is, of course, the predicament which now faces many of the e-commerce start-ups – though not the clicks and mortar entrants, whose prices will generally have been set in their existing, conventional markets.

Even in the case of the start-ups, the new product may be entering an existing market – one probably led by conventional delivery systems. If this is the case then price will only be one of the positioning variables. On this basis, the price should be carefully calculated to position the brand exactly where it will make the most impact and profit. At a less sophisticated level, perhaps, the producer of a new brand will decide which of the existing price ranges, cheap or expensive, the product or service should address. A supplier entering a traditional market can simply go to the local supermarket or speciality store and see what prices are already accepted. For e-commerce it is even simpler – just search the web without leaving your desk! In industrial markets it may be more difficult to obtain competitive prices, even where published price lists are available, since these are often only the starting point for negotiations which result in heavy discounts – IBM's dealers, for example, were often willing to offer up to a 35% discount against list price. This was the case even for a product which was in short supply, which is an indication of the problems which can be faced in a suicidally competitive market, which e-commerce can be.

With a new product or service, which may apply to some of the new e-commerce start-ups (though to far fewer than the hype might suggest), the pricing exercise will be that much more difficult, for there will no precedents to indicate how the consumer might behave, and this is an area where market research is notoriously inaccurate. In the end it will have to be a judgment decision as to what 'perceived value' the consumer will put on the offering.

In this position, there are two main approaches possible for a new product, and to a lesser extent for an existing one:

 **GETTING STARTED**

I *Skimming* – one approach is to set the initial price high, to 'skim' off as much profit as possible, even in the early stages of the product life cycle. In theory, this is an option open to all products or services, and indeed is an option which can apply throughout the life of the product – assuming that the producer adopts a policy of limited competition, for example niche marketing. It is particularly applicable to new products which, at least for a time, have a monopoly of the market because the competitors have not yet emerged.

This is a pattern often seen in the introduction of new technology such as video recorders and single lens reflex cameras – though it has not yet been seen much in e-commerce.

The initial price is kept high in order to make the maximum profit from the initially limited demand and probably equally limited supplies. It is then reduced, possibly in stages to gradually expand demand, until it reaches a competitive level just before the competitors enter the market. This is a fine judgment, though, and it is interesting to note that in the case of the video recorders and cameras mentioned above it was the late-comers, who had competitive prices, who actually swept the board!

The rationale behind the 'skimming' policy (sometimes called 'rapid payback') is quite simply that of maximising profit. But there may occasionally be another motive – that of maximising the image of 'quality', in which case the policy of high pricing, to demonstrate quality, would also continue throughout the life of the product or service. This is a policy which holds in consumer markets such as the upper end of the perfume trade, where Chanel No. 5 probably would not increase its sales dramatically if the price was reduced. But this can just as easily apply in industrial markets. It is the foolish consultant who asks for a low price, because the client will probably think that the quality of the product is comparably low. It was said, even several decades ago, that McKinsey was so successful because they would not enter a company for less than $100,000, which meant that the company had to take them, and their quality, seriously.

As indicated above, the danger of a skimming policy is that a high price encourages other manufacturers to enter the market because they see that sales revenue can quickly cover the expense of developing a rival product. While launch costs can be relatively low in most e-commerce markets, this is a danger which cannot be ignored. Even if your prices are not exorbitant you may still need, therefore, to plan for a steady reduction in price as competitors appear and you recover some of your launch costs. Figure 7.3 illustrates the 'skimming' policy.

> **KEY CONCEPT**
> ───────────
> The most prevalent new product pricing policy now is aimed at 'penetration'.

2 *Penetration policy* – on the other hand a manufacturer could choose the opposite tactic by adopting a penetration pricing policy, and this was very successful in the 1970s and 1980s, behind the move of the Japanese corporations into a number of existing markets, including those of the later stages of the introduction of video recorders and single lens reflex cameras. Here the price is set deliberately low, with a number of objectives in mind. The initial low price might make it less attractive for would-be competitors to imitate innovations, particularly where the technology is expensive. It encourages more customers to buy the product soon after its introduction – which hastens the growth of demand and earlier economies of scale. The main value of this policy is that it helps to seize a relatively large market share and increase turnover

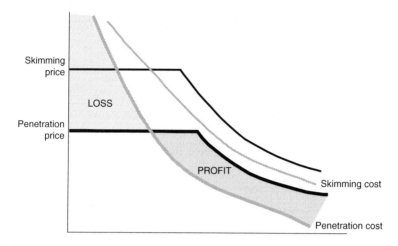

Figure 7.3: An illustration of 'skimming'

whilst (on the basis of economies of scale) reducing unit costs, so that the price domination can be maintained and extended. Its major disadvantage lies in losing the opportunity for higher profit margins. With 'competition' being the most prevalent strategy in the 1990s, however, penetration pricing has almost become the norm for a wide range of markets. It certainly seems to be the case for a high proportion of those in e-commerce! More important, perhaps, with relatively low launch costs it is likely to remain the model for future launches as well.

Vital questions and answers

- Does your organisation choose a 'skimming' policy for its new products? If so, what risks does this run – in terms of competitive entry?
- Does your organisation choose penetration pricing for its new products?

Overall, the most productive approach to pricing is to see it as the natural outcome of the *positioning process*.

Promotion

Moving on to the next of the traditional 4Ps, promotion, there is a range of alternative (and often complementary) vehicles available in conventional markets for *promoting* the product or service, and I will look at these first, to set the scene.

As a very direct approach, there is face-to-face sales. At the other extreme, there is the much more indirect approach, when it is too expensive to confront the customer personally, of advertising, or the even more indirect one of public

> **KEY CONCEPT**
>
> The promotional lozenge is a graphical approach to examining the balance between different promotional efforts.

relations. Finally, there is the immediate approach of sales (point of sale) promotion – which, if the reports are to be believed, now accounts for the largest part of the spend on promotion as a whole. To put these in a more memorable context than the amorphous 'promotional mix' (even though that does convey exactly what is involved) I like to look at it as a 'promotion lozenge' (Figure 7.4). It is shaped like a diamond, but I prefer to call it a lozenge because it can easily be moulded to fit the specific situation!

This lozenge is not as arbitrary as it may seem. It is actually organised along two dimensions. The vertical one should be obvious. It is the move from *indirect* (advertising) to *direct* (sales) contact with the customer.

Perhaps less obvious, but in many respects more important, is the horizontal dimension. This shows the flow over time, from the start with the establishment of a general interest via public relations (PR) through investment in image-building with advertising and much of the selling process, to the immediate impact of sales promotional devices

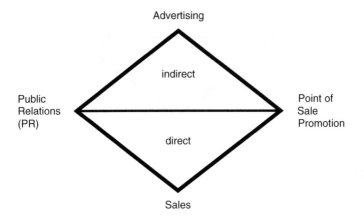

Figure 7.4: The promotion lozenge

at the point of sale. It also demonstrates the gradation from the long-term investment in PR and advertising/sales to the short-term effect of promotion.

The demands posed by your product/service package determine the shape of the lozenge; this is the reason for choosing a soft, malleable lozenge rather than a hard diamond. If you need the face-to-face (sales) contact to explain a complex package, and the price of this is sufficiently high to cover the high costs this implies, then the lozenge becomes almost an inverted triangle, such as shown in Figure 7.5.

The advertising element is almost missing, though even in the pure sales environment there will remain some element of indirect contact – often in the form of direct mail, to generate prospects for the face-to-face contact. The 'point of sale' here is a time (not a place), and the promotional element is usually only seen in the form of discounting the price. Despite my earlier comments, though, sales professionals would argue that this does need to have a very sharp cutting edge.

Almost the exact reverse occurs for fast-moving consumer goods where the low unit price means that face-to-face selling is simply not an economic proposition (Figure 7.6).

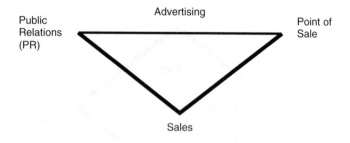

Figure 7.5: Emphasising the sales aspect of the lozenge

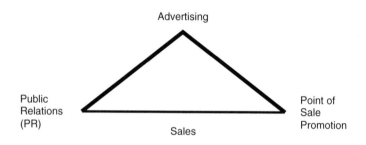

Figure 7.6: Emphasising the advertising aspect of the lozenge

Here 'sales' almost drops out of the picture, but not totally – for someone has to persuade distribution chains to carry the product/service package to the 'point of sale' (which here is a place, not a time). On the other hand, most of the effort must by necessity be invested in indirect communications. Once again, though, the promotion (here used at the point of sale) is very short-term – again usually in the form of some price reduction (either direct or indirect).

You can play many different games with the lozenge, but I will finish with conventional markets by showing one which is distorted to show – quite realistically – advertising (for, say, a consumer durable or a car) preceding face-to-face sales activity (in a retail outlet) (Figure 7.7).

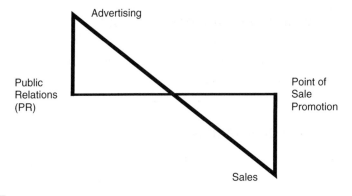

Figure 7.7: The distorted lozenge

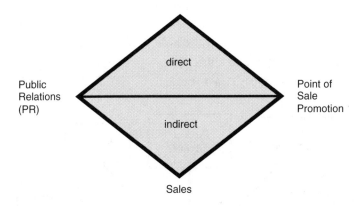

Figure 7.8: E-commerce covers the whole lozenge

We now move to the punch-line, which shows the power of e-commerce. As indicated in Figure 7.8, e-commerce covers the *whole* lozenge. Indeed, it can at any time be located *anywhere* in the lozenge – and then immediately move to anywhere else within it, as needed by the promotional tactics! This degree of flexibility can be immensely powerful, if used properly. But, once more, this has been largely ignored by most of the e-commerce players.

📝 **Vital questions and answers**

- Draw the equivalent lozenge for your own e-commerce offerings.

Advertising believability

There is one dimension of advertising which is too often forgotten – the *believability* of the various promotional messages (Figure 7.9).

The inputs to the believability equation are many, and – as can be seen from the figure – in traditional markets often lie outside of the advertising itself, so that the whole process is complex and difficult to manage. These outside factors

> **KEY CONCEPT**
>
> To be effective, advertising must be believable in terms of everything involved, from the organisation itself to the medium chosen.

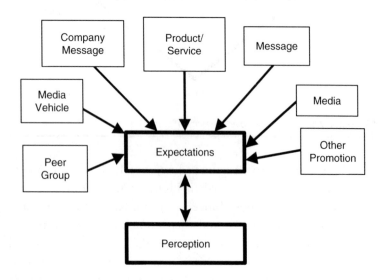

Figure 7.9: Possible promotional messages

often place limitations on what may reasonably be said within the advertisement itself. On the other hand, because e-commerce is also comprehensive and tightly integrated with the product/service being offered, it can be much better managed. Even so, the rule that satisfaction equals perception minus expectation must be observed. If you *expect* a certain level of service and *perceive* the service received to be higher, you will be a satisfied customer. If you perceive this same level of service where you had expected a higher one, you will be disappointed and therefore a dissatisfied customer.

Laws of service

David Maister[15] formulated two *Laws of Service*. The first of these is expressed by the formula hinted at above: 'Satisfaction equals perception minus expectation.' If you expect a certain level of service and perceive the service received to be higher, you will be a satisfied customer. If you perceive this same level where you had expected a higher one, you will be disappointed and therefore a dissatisfied customer. Figure 7.10 shows what makes customers satisfied and dissatisfied.

The important point is that both what is perceived and what is expected are psychological phenomena – not reality – and it is the *relative* level of service – related to expectations – which is important, not the absolute one.

Most important of all is that the above equation does not just cover pre-purchase belief. Belief (expectations) is in practice satisfied by the offering – a highly believable message may cause serious problems when the product/service package fails to live up to it.

[15] Maister, D.H. (1988) The psychology of waiting lines. In *Managing Services: Marketing, Operations and Human Resources*, NJ, Prentice-Hall.

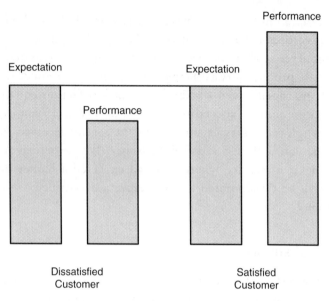

Figure 7.10: Customer satisfaction and dissatisfaction

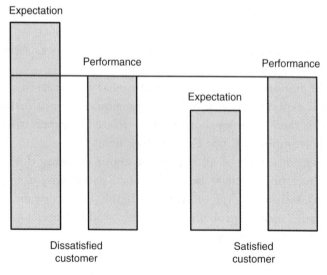

Figure 7.11: Customer satisfaction and dissatisfaction (controlling expectation levels)

Because so much information is available to the purchaser on a website, as opposed to being swayed by the few words of a conventional mass media advertisement, this may be less of a problem in e-commerce; since the buyer should already be aware of the true situation.

 Vital questions and answers

- Are you promising more than you can deliver — and, in the subsequent dissatisfaction, are you risking losing the trust of your customers?
- Or are you promising less than you can deliver, and risking them never buying your offering?

Customer complaints

At the other end of the purchasing process, complaints are often treated as a nuisance. Indeed, many e-commerce organisations are so determined to avoid them that they exclude any means by which customers can make complaints! Yet complaints have considerable value for a number of reasons:

1   Although there will always be a small proportion of 'frivolous' complaints, a complaint usually highlights something which has gone wrong with a part of the overall marketing operation: usually the high quality which should be a fundamental requirement for most organisations has not been achieved. Whatever the reason, the sensible marketer will want to know exactly what has gone wrong so that remedial action may be taken. One strength of e-commerce is that its interactive nature enables the necessary conversations with the complainant

to take place easily, and in good time, and the flexible nature of the 'product' allows for remedies to be quickly applied.

2   The way a complaint is handled is often seen by customers, and their many contacts, as an acid test of the true quality of support. What is more, it is also a powerful reminder to the organisation's own staff of just how important quality is.

3   *Customers who complain are usually loyal customers* (those who are not loyal tend just to switch to another supplier), and will continue to be loyal (and valuable) customers – so long as their complaint is handled well.

In e-commerce the transparent nature of the processes themselves provide reassurance. Even so, the following should be borne in mind.

 IMPLEMENTATION CHECKLIST

1   *The first requirement is that complaints should be positively encouraged.* That is not the same as saying that the reasons for complaints should be encouraged. But, assuming that despite your best efforts a problem has occurred, you should put nothing in the way of any customer who wants to complain and, indeed, you should positively encourage such complaints – since the main problem lies with the many more customers who do not complain (and instead change to another supplier) rather than the few who abuse the complaints system. This may be difficult to achieve in conventional markets, where the face-to-face contact often relies on the member of staff causing the complaint to log it! It should be much easier in e-commerce, where a specific structure can be put in place which is guaranteed to work.

2 *The second requirement is that all complaints should be carefully handled by painstakingly controlled and monitored procedures.* Complaints must be handled well, and must be seen to be handled well; by the complainant and by the organisation's own staff. Again, the structure of an e-commerce system should easily ensure that the best audit trails are maintained, and regularly monitored.

3 *The third, and most important, requirement is that the complaint should then be fully investigated, and the cause remedied.* Complaints are only symptoms. The underlying disease needs to be cured. There may be an understandable temptation to overlook complaints until they reach a 'significant' level – but holding off until the complaints reach this level usually means that they have already become damaging to the organisation's image. It is far better to assume that 'one complaint is too many'.

The reality in most organisations is very different. Despite the ease with which complaints may be handled, e-commerce companies are perhaps the worst offenders – possibly because the customer is remote, and has no means of embarrassing the manager responsible. Too often the number of complaints are minimised not by remedying the reasons for them but by evading the complainants.

> **KEY CONCEPT**
>
> Customer complaints are an opportunity to demonstrate service to loyal customers.

The assumption is usually made, wrongly so, that complainants are trouble-makers; and have to be handled in a confrontational manner.

The reality is that most dissatisfied customers do not complain (a US survey[16] showed that 97% didn't), but they do tell their friends (the same survey showed that 13%

[16] Albrecht, K. and Zemke, R. (1985) *Service America*, New York, Dow-Jones Irwin.

complained to more than 20 other people). In e-commerce markets it is easy to avoid an unsatisfactory vendor – there are many others to choose from, just a click or so away – and then you can tell the whole

world (or large parts of it) about your unhappy experience. Clearly, if it was not already obvious, any organisation should be highly motivated to make certain its customers are satisfied. Yet, in practice, remarkably few do so.

 ## Vital questions and answers

- A useful exercise, if you can get permission for it, is to make a dummy complaint to your own organis- ation, and see what happens! But you may have difficulty in gaining permission, or may be told to warn the people involved first, for almost nothing worries most organisations more than the possibility of finding out that their complaints processes don't work.

Satisfaction surveys

Following this train of thought, it is *essential* that an organisation monitors the satisfaction level of its customers. This may be at the global level, as measured by market research. Preferably, though, it should be at the level of individuals or groups – especially where this is easy to achieve, by simply asking customers, after they have used the service, how satisfied they are.

IBM, at the peak of its success, conducted a survey of all its direct customers every year. The results were analysed not only to produce overall satisfaction indices, though that was done (and senior management viewed any deterioration with alarm), but they were also provided to field manage- ment so that they could rectify any

> **KEY CONCEPT**
>
> Satisfaction surveys unearth hidden problems and reassure customers.

individual problem situations – where the customer was dissatisfied with any aspect of the IBM service and the IBM representative (presumably in 97% of the occasions if the above results – of the numbers who do not complain – hold true in this field) did not realise this to be the case! Much the same can be done with individual e-commerce customers – something which is much more difficult in conventional marketing.

There are a number of advantages to conducting satisfaction surveys (particularly where any individual problems highlighted can be subsequently dealt with) for e- commerce as much as for traditional markets:

1 Like complaints, they indicate where problems lie for rectification.
2 If they cover all customers, they allow the 97% of non-complainers to communicate their feelings and vent their anger.
3 They show even satisfied customers that their supplier is interested in the customer and their complaints – which goes half-way to satisfying those complainants.
4 They help persuade the supplier's staff to take customer service more seriously.

The only difference with e-commerce is that the process should be much easier to undertake!

The importance of very high standards of customer service is evidenced by two examples. The marketing philosophy of

McDonalds, the world's largest food service organisation, is encapsulated in its motto 'Q.S.C.& V.' (Quality, Service, Cleanliness & Value). The standards, enforced somewhat quixotically (but memorably) on its franchisees and managers at the 'Hamburger University' in Elk Grove Village, Illinois, require that the customer receives a 'good-tasting' hamburger in no more than five minutes, from a friendly host or hostess, in a spotlessly clean restaurant. The second example, Disneyland, also insists on spotless cleanliness, and on the customer being 'The Guest'. It is salutary to observe how few competitors in either of these fields manage the simple task of keeping their premises clean, let alone being able to think of their customers as 'guests'. It is also illuminating that in the fairground trade (with which Disney competes, albeit at a very different level) customers are often seen as some form of victim ('pigeon', 'mark', 'punter' etc.) – to be fleeced before the fair moves on! E-commerce pioneers, with the important exception of Amazon, unfortunately seem to be following the latter path.

Vital questions and answers

- Think a while. How satisfied do you really think your customers might be? Also ask a friend, for a less biased view.

Services in e-commerce

CHAPTER 8

Overview

We now move on to briefly look at some of the other features of e-commerce which are significantly different to what has happened in traditional markets. For, as Daniel Amor[17] says, 'Content is King. The most important thing on your web page is content; never let users leave your web page without giving them information.' Indeed, that information may be the product itself. Thus, National Geographic invested in the purchase of Wildflower Productions (a specialist in printing maps on demand) in order to offer personalised recreation maps via the Internet. This chapter therefore sets out to introduce you to the main ways of providing these services.

At the same time you will want to make your site(s) easy to use. The content has little value if it cannot be accessed – and the customer will quickly click to another site where he can more easily find what he wants. Accordingly, this chapter looks at various devices, and services, which can be used to aid navigation and to build trust with your customers.

---

[17] Amor, D. (2000) *The e-Business (R)Evolution: living and working in an interconnected world*, NJ, Prentice-Hall.

CONTINUED . . . Overview

- Syndication
- Applications service providers (ASPs)
- Portals
- Tailoring
- Collaborative filtering
- Databases
- Navigation and spiders
- Guarantors
- Content brokers

Material content

You will want your website to offer the greatest amount of information to your customers. But you will probably also want to gain the maximum exposure, on other websites as well as your own, for the material you produce. Of course, you can always do both yourself, but one of the benefits of the web is that you can share – both ways – simply by hot-linking to other sites and by making your offering available on as many portals as possible. The most productive aspect of this is that, unlike physical industrial goods, information can – especially in this way – be used and reused, sold and resold, many times without incurring significant extra cost or losing value. Indeed, the new challenge to traditional economic theory is that knowledge actually becomes more valuable the more it is used!

Syndication

Fortunately, some new business models are becoming available to match the new moves which are leading to the

breakdown of barriers between organisations. Even before
e-commerce became so visible, at the end of the twentieth
century, reducing barriers meant that organisations were less
inclined to do everything in-house. In particular, they were
much happier to share their business with partners in a
number of fields. In a specific context of syndication it even
means that they are willing to allow partners in a distribution
chain to badge their products. This has long been the case in
terms of television programmes, especially in the US, where
the leading television shows have been distributed on a range
of channels and syndicated through them. Equally this has
been true, again especially in the US, of syndicated columns
in the popular press. It is starting to be the case with e-
commerce. For example, Amazon will happily provide you
with all their services under your own label. From Amazon's
point of view, as well as selling direct to individuals it can
also create thousands of further bookshops to whom it gives
a percentage commission – but whose business then adds to
its throughput.

Such syndication leads to three
different roles in the distribution
channel. These are the *originators*,
who in this way widen the range of
markets they can address whilst still
maintaining control of their standardised 'product', *distributors*, who
deliver it to the consumers, and – as a new addition –
syndicators, those organisations which specialise in packaging
the material and integrating it with that from other
originators.

> **KEY CONCEPT**
>
> Content of websites can
> be syndicated to and from
> other website owners and
> content distributors.

Other sorts of arrangements can apply to *affiliates* who, in
essence, claim discount for passing business through to the
original vendor. Even my own university, the Open University
in the UK, has in this way made several million pounds from
passing customers through to commercial affiliates.

Vital questions and answers

- Who might you be able to (profitably) syndicate some of your e-commerce offerings *to*?
- Who might you be able to (profitably) syndicate e-commerce offerings *from*?

Applications service providers (ASPs)

Using another – specialist – organisation to handle your e-commerce business, or part of it, can be an effective and easy way to enter e-commerce. Thus, at the other end of the spectrum from affiliates we have *applications service providers*, who take over the running of e-commerce applications for businesses, leasing applications, such as word processing, databases and enterprise resource planning to their clients via the Internet. They may take over parts of it by providing suitable software, for example to run the search engines. Indeed, the software search engines used by those sites which advertise themselves as directory providers (such as Yahoo!) are often now supplied by third parties, sometimes by the same one as their competitors!

Taking the process further, in the case of many smaller organisations, these ASPs may well take over the running of the website and the order fulfilment procedures. It is arguable that in this way they can initially cut costs by between 30 and 70%, with

> **KEY CONCEPT**
>
> ASPs can run most aspects of an e-commerce operation for you if need be.

the added benefit that the vendor doesn't have to spend significant amounts of time and attention on maintaining the site – even though it is still to be kept at the leading edge of technology. On the other hand, the running costs can eventually be 20–30% higher, and your business may come to depend upon those ASPs! So the best advice is to use such ASPs in setting up your initial e-commerce applications, but not to allow them to get a stranglehold on your e-business. Ultimately you are likely to want to go it alone.

 Vital questions and answers

- Do you use ASPs?
- Do you use ASPs to completely manage your site(s)?
- If so, what are you doing to ensure that you can still become independent at a later stage?

Portals

Taking this approach to its logical extreme, some organisations are now billing themselves as portals. A portal is simply a (web)site which offers itself as a starting (entry) point for Internet users wanting to connect to the Internet, or it is an 'anchor site' which is visited regularly by them. But some organisations are also starting to claim that they can offer the whole range of services, to a wide range of customers, under one entry point – in particular under one brand. In essence, they want to become the customer's one-stop shop for everything. For example, Yahoo! has already adopted such an approach and even eBay is aspiring to it.

In this way, such sites aim to provide the widest range of possible services, either from within their own resources or, increasingly, by hot-linking to other service providers. The original portals, such as AOL – which has now merged with Time-Warner, to enhance its media based offerings, and CompuServe,

> **KEY CONCEPT**
>
> Portals aim to release the great value created by their relationship with members.

which now runs its business offerings – have since been joined by hundreds of other portals, all trying to jump on the same bandwagon. The most important of these new additions are, at one extreme, those now offering to provide 'free' links to the Internet, such as Freeserve, although the financial realities of this are gradually forcing even these to introduce charges for their members. At the other extreme are directories and search engines, such as Yahoo!, which now also offer the full range of services. Other specialists are those (such as GeoCities, now part of Yahoo!), which offer a range of neighbourhoods where you can find people with similar interests to your own.

Most of these portals now syndicate services from other providers, or hot-link to them. Their main advantage is that – at virtually no extra operating costs – they integrate these separate offerings under one simple-to-use umbrella. There are two main types of portal: 'horizontal portals', like AOL and Freeserve, which aim to offer almost everything to a wide range of customers (as one-stop shops), and 'vertical portals', like Amazon, which are more tightly focused on a specific audience.

There is a long way to go before these putative portals achieve their objectives, but in the longer term it is possible that they may be a very valuable investment. Thus, while it is not clear what their radical new products may be, their real value may well come from their ownership of affinity groups. In other words, the more members, or at least the more loyal members you have, the more valuable the package you have to offer. In this respect you can almost put a value on each member. At the height of the e-commerce boom, AOL members, for example, seem to have been valued at around $15,000 each. The financial numbers have since become much more realistic but the principle is still the same. The value is, in some mysterious way, locked into the numbers of members you have. Except that it isn't really mysterious. The sales of whatever you have, in terms of products or services, will be proportional to the numbers of loyal members you have. Portal owners are currently trying to make their money from banner advertising sold to vendors promoting their products, services and websites. Again, to generate sufficient income, this needs a large number of visitors.

 Vital questions and answers

- How many 'members', for your e-commerce services do you have? . . . . . .
- How many *loyal* 'members', for your e-commerce services do you have? . . . . . .
- Using a possible value of $2000 for each loyal member, what asset value does this imply? $ . . . . . .

Making e-services easy to use

The first point to make about any e-service you provide is that it *must* be responsive. This sounds obvious, but Chris Voss[18] found that, in practice, it was often far from instantaneous, as Figure 8.1 shows.

Assuming there is a timely response, one thing that any Internet site must achieve, if it is to be successful, is ease of use. It's not like normal retail, for example, where even in the supermarket you have human beings to help – albeit only in the form of cashiers or greeters. On the Web you are *all alone.* Alone and lost, there is no one to ask. One of the first Internet failures, Boo.com, was supposed to have failed

---

[18] Voss, C. (2000) Developing an e-service strategy. *Business Strategy Review* **11** (1), 21–33.

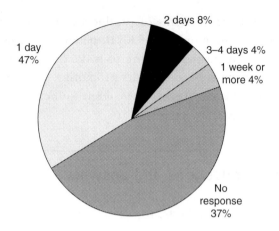

Figure 8.1: Response times to e-mail enquiries

precisely because – as a retailer of fashion goods – it was too complex to use.

In particular, it was very slow – it took anything up to half an hour to order an item. In using the Internet, people want to be able to click immediately on any item they need, and anything that takes more than 30 seconds to download risks being abandoned.

But, in addition to providing the fastest possible response, website design has to ensure that you *can't* get lost and then it has to provide ways of rescuing you when you *do* get lost. It should ultimately allow you access to a human being who can provide you with advice (something that many websites do not even consider).

Chris Voss suggests some ways to ease navigation, including the following:

1 **Restricting** the amount of information on the screen presented to users.
2 **Grouping** users so that they can go direct to the part of the site they need.

3 **Developing** ways of navigating that make sense to users and providing logical routes to the data.

 Vital questions and answers

■ How does your own site rate in terms of users being able to easily navigate their way around it: Easy navigation/Poor navigation/Almost impossible to use?

Tailoring

Perhaps the most productive approach is to tailor your website to the individual customer. This may be in terms of tailoring content, in the way that Amazon offers tailored suggestions for its book purchasers. Or it may be in terms of offering a different choice of content, or better still it might be in terms of knowing more about your customers in terms of clothing sizes, etc.

This means that individual users provide a profile of themselves, and this is used – possibly by some form of artificial intelligence – to shape the question and answer sessions that they are exposed to in buying the service or

> **KEY CONCEPT**
>
> Tailoring your website to the individual customer visiting it is the most productive approach.

product to ensure that many of the 'admin' questions will already have been answered. Best of all, though not yet readily available, it will know how you like to use the web itself. Thus, you should be able to tailor the website – as you see it – to the way that you want to use it. It could be that you would prefer to search by menu, by index or by words. The ideal website would offer you a choice of which route to follow. The value of this has yet to be demonstrated in practice: according to Sandeep *et al.*,[19] '. . . fewer than 15 per cent of visitors to Yahoo! have chosen to set up a "My Yahoo" page for themselves.' However, if you actually look at this facility on Yahoo!, you will find that it is both difficult to set up and unproductive to use, so perhaps it is a bad example, and more worthwhile ones will succeed.

At the very least, the website should know about the customer's personal details and in particular their credit card details. This means that when they place an order, as is the case with Amazon, *all they need do is validate (electronically 'sign') that order*, and the website will fill in the rest of the details. Of course, this raises questions of privacy. Customers have to trust the website owner to carefully guard your details. In addition, this often means that, again as in the case of Amazon, the website places a 'cookie' on their own customers' computers, so that when they talk to the website it immediately knows all about them. That cookie, in fact, is usually a customer number, so only that website can link into that customer's personal details.

> **KEY CONCEPT**
>
> All a customer need do to order should be to validate it with one click.

Even so, as a vendor, you should be aware that some users will still object to even this amount of intrusion into their privacy. But, of course, you can give them the alternative of not accepting this approach and having to insert their personal details each time they place an order. Again, it's horses for courses. If you are very clever as a website owner, you can link people's purchases to those of other purchasers with a similar profile – in particular to those with a similar purchase profile. Amazon regularly updates each customer's

[19] Sandeep, D., Landesberg, H. and Zeisser, M. (2000) Building digital brands. *The McKinsey Quarterly* 2.

profile by seeing what *similar* purchasers are now doing and buying. The great advantage of this is that it is based on the latest information; those purchasers are now buying new books that are coming out – and Amazon can immediately link others to that pattern. Based on their ordering, it will suggest which new books might be suitable for similar customers.

Collaborative filtering

Alternatively, in matching your offer to user wants, you can make use of a similar technique, pioneered by Firefly (now owned by Microsoft). Consumers' opinions (given on a questionnaire) and choices are compared with those of other users. Based upon statistical matches, the choices of similar customers are used to predict suitable choices of movies, records etc., and these are then offered to the customer, as *automatic customisation*. On the other hand, *manual customisation* may be simply achieved by asking customers to identify the content they wish to use by check boxes or pull-down menus. This is an approach used by news services.

Tailoring and databases

The technical resources needed for this sort of processing relate to the associated database handling operations. This is a complex subject, especially as some of the databases may be very large indeed. Taken one element at a time it may seem simple to match you with a suitable product, but with many millions of elements and very varied customer profiles the requirement may demand the most sophisticated pieces of software now being developed. As a result, the topic is beyond the scope of this book! The best advice is simply to take the best advice – find database experts, who you trust, to do the work for you.

One of the major benefits of the Internet as a whole is that you can allow much wider access for your customers to crucial data that you hold yourself. Thus for, example, FedEx (Federal Express) allow their customers to track the parcels they have sent in FedEx's computer system. Other competitors now offer the same service. This takes a significant load off administration staff, but more importantly, it gives customers the feeling that they are in control of what's happening, and that is a major competitive advantage.

Vital questions and answers

- Do you maintain customer profiles?
- Do you tailor elements on your site to take advantage of such profiles?
- How do you do this?

Navigators and spiders

Before we leave the subject of websites, it is worth noting that it is not just your customers who may be looking for your website. Crawlers (sometimes known as spiders) are also sent around the web by the main search engine sites. These catalogue websites and make them available, through the search engines, to anyone who asks them suitable questions. To provide this guidance, most of the major search engines (including AltaVista, Excite, HotBot, Infoseek and Lycos) use the 'spiders' (also known as robots, e-bots or wanderers) which travel the web automatically visiting websites, studying them and then reporting back to their owners. Yahoo! adds human intervention to look at submissions (and to create a hierarchy) when developing its index. A number of sites (including AOL and Lycos) now use the Inktomi engine (covering 500 million pages) although in mid-2000 Yahoo! switched from it to Google (which covers more than one billion pages) to drive their search facilities, since Google, having entered the market late decided that its superior technical capabilities were best used by selling them on – in a classic example of the new forms of syndication which are possible on the Internet.

The key to obtaining the best coverage by these directories is making your web site crawler-friendly as well as user-friendly. Fortunately this is easy. You should make your first paragraph of text as explicit as possible, and as comprehensive as possible, using

> **KEY CONCEPT**
>
> Sites are catalogued by search engine (navigator/ spider) software.

in it as many words as you can to describe your site, its content and purpose, because web-crawlers usually do not go much beyond the start of a website before they decide how it can be catalogued or classified under their various headings. Even more important, the metatags that live in the HTML code at the top of the page must also be as succinct and as comprehensive as possible. These are the things that crawlers look for. I had the experience, in the early days after launching my first website, of wondering why no one could seem to find it – only to discover that my IT staff had put as the only metatag the single word 'index'. This is one of the words the web-crawlers are explicitly told to ignore. Hence my whole website was ignored! You should ensure that as many keywords and phrases as possible have been added to the metatags on your website.

 Vital questions and answers

■ Do you make special provisions to allow for spiders?

New services

In the context of one-to-one *networking*, a whole range of other organisations will also be needed to provide the various new services that these demand. This section will discuss these organisations in more detail.

Guarantors

I have already mentioned 'trust' several times. In terms of physical products this is built upon the experience of the user, over the lifetime of the product(s) they buy. Even before they are bought,

> **KEY CONCEPT**
>
> Guarantors are needed to underwrite trust in unknown servicers.

prospective purchasers can touch them to see how they feel (and quality is often, irrationally, judged by weight). As you will no doubt already have learned, similar levels of trust are more difficult to build for services, where you cannot touch the product. Even so, over time, successive service encounters gradually build levels of trust, though these are very susceptible to even one unsatisfactory service encounter. Something similar is likely to apply to those Internet businesses which can build on multiple contacts with their customers: Amazon, for instance, is very aware of this – hence its 'no questions asked' returns policy.

But one major attraction of the Internet is its ability to deliver individual-to-individual contacts between literally millions of users. It is unlikely that trust can be built here upon multiple contacts and, in any case, an unsatisfactory first contact such as a fraud (as eBay management, with its caveat emptor policy, admit already permeate their auction services) could be damaging to the customer. So, in order to enable commercial transactions to take place in the wider e-commerce environment, some intermediaries who underpin that trust will need to be created.

The banks are already looking to provide means of certificating transactions, so that the money which changes hands over the Internet is protected. That, in fact, is probably the easiest part of the process; the remaining part of the transaction – establishing whether the product and, in particular, the service is of good quality – may be much harder to achieve. Where there are literally millions of vendors around the world it will be very difficult to track them all, and where fraud is already evident, people may well think twice before buying from unknown, unseen vendors. One recent attempt at handling this, through guilds of suppliers (being set up by NatWest Bank, under the title of IQport) unfortunately foundered – but the idea was that these guarantors would be licensed by central authority (in this example, by the commercial organisation, NatWest).

 Vital questions and answers

- How do you 'guarantee' your offering(s)?
- Do you, deliberately or by default, use outside organisations to underwrite your offerings?
- If so, what is their role and how is this managed by you?

Content brokers

Another set of organisations are starting to offer various pieces of the content which websites use to attract customers. For example, Virgin.net offer the

KEY CONCEPT

Content brokers may be able to offer all the content you need to provide interest for your site.

product (and services) of more than 100 entertainment-oriented organisations within the Virgin empire. It will offer them to you, to badge as being owned by your site, so that your purchasers have access to that content. Clearly, if you are aiming to be a one-stop shop (as a portal), you will be very interested in bringing on board the maximum number of content providers, and may use wholesalers of content, the content brokers, as part of this. Equally, however, you may in turn sell on that content: becoming in the process a content broker yourself. The relationships at this stage of the game get very muddy indeed, and it will often be difficult to say whether an organisation is a portal, an information vendor, a content broker, a membership club or something else.

 Vital questions and answers

- Do you buy in content *from* outside providers?
- Do you sell content *to* other organisations?
- What is your strategy for such content transfers?

The e-retail model

CHAPTER 9

Overview

This part of the book is significantly longer than the economics of e-retail (or e-tail, as it is sometimes now called) justifies. The reason for this is that it is a particularly good model for looking at e-commerce in general. This is because, using it, we can remove the complexities introduced by the intangible services element. For e-retail, we can talk about 'product' as if it is only a physical product. This doesn't mean, of course, that this is always the case. Indeed, today it is only likely to be the case – even in consumer markets – some of the time. But it does mean that we can see more clearly the distribution (channel) implications of e-commerce.

The aims and objectives of this chapter are therefore:

♦ To investigate how *traditional theory* and techniques might apply, and what changes might be needed, in the context of *retailing*.

♦ To put *consumer e-marketing* in the context of *direct marketing*, both from the historical perspective and that of likely future developments.

♦ To use the lessons from this specific (e-retail) sector as a *model* for e-commerce in general, and B2C (business-to-consumer) in particular.

CONTINUED . . . Overview

- Fulfilment
- Disintermediation
- Price comparisons
- One-stop shops
- Clicks and mortar
- Organisational cultures
- e-retail product decisions
- Range, place, promotion, merchandising
- Databases
- Direct marketing
- Electronic catalogues
- Mailings
- Clubs
- Personal profiles
- Direct advertising
- Lists
- Direct offers

E-retail

One of the advantages of exploring e-retail is that there is a very long history of direct marketing, if not of e-commerce, in this field.

Thus the first evidence of the new techniques involved came – as you might expect – with a new technology. On the other hand, the new technology was the creation of the US mail service. In 1887, Sears

> **KEY CONCEPT**
>
> E-retail represents an easy to understand 'model' of e-commerce in general.

Roebuck started its catalogue operations, which are still used as a model for modern e-commerce ventures such as Amazon.

Over the years this sector has grown. In fact, the range of other operators that depend upon catalogues is still steadily growing, from small companies selling fishing gear or lingerie to the equivalent of department stores selling everything. Although the original Sears Roebuck catalogue was comprehensive (going as far as including buggies, the deluxe cars of the period), the most modern *printed* catalogues are works of art – hundreds of pages long with beautiful colour photographs. It is arguable that their equivalent on the web is rather less impressive, because of the limitations of downloading such high-quality pictures.

Fulfilment

In terms of physical product, also, not much has changed. Amazon still uses a very similar delivery process. The order may be placed slightly differently, though for some time catalogue operators have been taking orders over the telephone – and this process was not too different to those now arriving over the Internet. Thereafter, these orders are picked in a warehouse, or supplied by the vendor, and delivered to the end-user by mail – or more likely these days by FedEx or another courier company.

There was initially a great belief in 'virtual marketing', whereby Amazon thought it had discovered the economic miracle of not holding any stocks and passing all work on to its vendors. It very quickly found that, while its vendors were quite capable of shipping pallets of material to Amazon, they could not handle parcels which needed to be sent to individual customers. So Amazon had to spend billions of dollars on setting up its own warehousing distribution system more suited to the needs of e-commerce.

> **KEY CONCEPT**
>
> E-commerce fulfilment may be different in that it involves parcel deliveries to individual homes.

This caused a major financial hiccup for Amazon. The challenge is having a delivery system which handles small parcels well – to individuals – as did the original Sears Roebuck operation through the US mail. It cannot rely upon volume delivery of pallet loads to supermarkets, which until recently the modern distribution system revolved around.

 Vital questions and answers

- How does your own organisation handle, or propose to handle, the fulfilment logistics of its e-commerce operations?
- How does/will it address the problem of delivering small parcels to individual homes?

Disintermediation

Much has been said about the changes that are being made to the overall distribution chain, and a considerable amount of jargon is thrown around as well. One of these pieces of jargon is 'disintermediation'. All this means is that, because of the possibility of direct contact with the customer, several stages in the distribution chain can be cut out.

Thus, Amazon has cut out the bookshops and now sells direct to the end-user. As I have already indicated, this was nothing new, since catalogue operators have been doing this for decades. But – as these catalogue operations showed – companies may merely be transferring some costs (of space on a high street) to another area (of delivering the

KEY CONCEPT

Disintermediation means that e-commerce is used to cut out the middle-men.

catalogue to consumers, and having the order fulfilment process which can match this).

But the advent of e-commerce has allowed this sort of operation to move into new areas. In particular, Dell has used direct marketing – to end users in organisations around the world – to revolutionise the personal computer market. By focusing on individual customers (often managers and professionals) at their desks, Dell has managed to reduce the costs involved (which is probably the first justification for such an operation), but has also improved the speed of response (and in the process reduced Dell's stock holding), and also the choice, since customers can order PCs to be built to their exact specification. This example nicely illustrates many of the one-to-one strengths of such direct marketing operations in e-commerce.

 Vital questions and answers

- How have your distribution channels been changed by e-commerce?
- What strategy have you adopted to allow for, and capitalise on, these changes?

Price comparisons

In the first stages, at least, the great benefit for the customer was supposed to come from the ability of consumers to cross-compare prices. This, in many respects, goes against the concept of one-to-one marketing, which ought to be about matching to individual requirements. On the other hand, it is certainly true that it is much easier to compare prices, and with various intelligent agents roaming the net you no longer even have to do this yourself. So in certain markets the result has been that commodity pricing has been brought into play – although the reality is much less dramatic than the hype allows for. The result is that a number of operators, including those in the retail arena, have seen very small margins – and often losses. On the other hand, this is no different to many other price war situations in traditional markets.

One-stop shopping

At the other end of the spectrum the claim is often made that Internet shopping can be all about convenience – the customer can find, on one site even (where that is the claim of some of the new portals), everything he or she might want. They never need put a foot outside their own front door. This is indeed a convenience for some consumers, and a few supermarkets – for instance – have set up operations allowing people to place orders from their desk at work, which can then be picked up in the car park as they leave in the evening. This is certainly a new addition to convenience shopping, but it may not be a major benefit for all, or even most consumers. Thus, 24-hour conventional shopping might be just as advantageous, especially as the superstores involved have to keep their facilities open and staff employed through the night as they restock the shelves. Accordingly, they might be able to do some extra business for little extra cost.

 Vital questions and answers

- At which end of the spectrum do your e-commerce operations lie – commodity prices, one-stop shopping, or specialised/luxury goods/services?

Clicks and mortar

Another of the controversies which is more easily seen in terms of e-retail is that of existing businesses versus new start-ups. Existing businesses moving into the field, particularly in e-retail (where the term seems to have started) are referred to as 'clicks and mortar'. The idea is that they have the clicks of the e-commerce side and the mortar from their traditional high-street businesses.

The initial feeling, or at least the hype, was that the start-up businesses would walk all over these existing retailers. They didn't have the high overheads caused by investments in space and buildings that the existing retailers had. Indeed, some of the existing retailers, such as Sainsbury, have actually gone as far as to set up separate e-retail operations to service this market – so that they can gain all the supposed benefits of the more efficient logistics. In reality, this doesn't appear to have been the case (apart from with Amazon which gained a significant first-mover advantage), since existing company infrastructure has proved to be sufficiently flexible in many cases. For example, Tesco has used its existing physical infrastructure to meet the demands of its e-commerce business, and this gave it a head-start over its competitors, and actually seems to have reduced costs, not increased them. Sainsbury has now also added this approach to its more specialised, warehouse-based, operations. There also had to be some innovations. Tesco, for example (www.tesco.com), still had to find a suitable means of delivering to the customer's house, and this is no mean achievement when these days – with both partners working – the customer is rarely at home!

> **KEY CONCEPT**
>
> The most profitable operators may be those who extend traditional businesses, which have already covered their overhead costs, into e-commerce.

It was claimed that e-commerce would undermine the supermarkets. The recent move to huge out-of-town supermarkets, which necessitated taking the car to go shopping, had favoured these superstores. But it was hoped that the power of the supermarkets would be broken by e-commerce. That clearly hasn't happened, perhaps because the supermarkets have had the financial muscle available to move into the new markets. However, I suspect it is too early for them to rest on their laurels. The operating requirements – and even the culture – of e-commerce will almost certainly change the retailing experience for many people and, in such a changing environment, it is always the existing brand leaders that are put under the greatest stress – but equally they have the greatest financial muscle to deal with the changes.

Culture

The main problem the *existing* retailers, and other businesses, will face is simply that of being locked in to their *existing culture*. If you have many years of history behind you, selling on the high street for example, you will have consider-

> **KEY CONCEPT**
>
> There may be culture clashes between the traditional and e-commerce sides of a business.

able difficulty learning the new skills – and there are many new skills needed – for trading on the Internet. You may also find considerable resistance coming from your staff who have, over the years, built up significant attitudes about what constitutes the service they provide. Often these reflect what enhances the position of members of staff rather than what is really good for the customer. There is a great deal of inertia in existing businesses, which is very difficult to break down. There may even be conflicts of interest. If you have, as many organisations have, partners in the existing distribution chains then they may object to you – in effect – opening up a major new distribution chain through e-commerce. Levi's, the jeans manufacturer, for example, found this to be the case when they tried to sell jeans via the Internet – members of their existing distribution chain virtually went on strike.

 Vital questions and answers

- Can your organisation use both clicks and mortar?
- How do you manage the potential clash between the two cultures?

E-retail organisation

I won't go into any significant detail here about the differences between different types of retail operation, e-commerce or not, except to highlight the significant changes which may be likely to take place at the lower levels of organisational life. The multinationals will probably carry on as normal: they have the resources to take on board e-commerce as part of business as usual. The companies that may benefit most though, may be at the other end of the chain, the small – independent – suppliers. It is arguable that they can take their existing offerings, which may be very local, and offer them to the world as a whole for very little extra investment. One of the most dubious elements of the hype about Internet start-ups was the talk of hundreds of millions of pounds being needed for such launches. Indeed, for some very odd reasons, that was what at one stage the financial markets said they were worth. Even then, underneath the surface, although they were spending money like water, their actual start-up costs were low by modern standards. Thus, at least one survey has shown that most of the organisations which knew what they were spending on their Internet operations thought that their investment was less than £35,000. By far the greatest majority simply didn't know what it was – which is understandable where £35,000 is small beer to most organisations. *In other words, starting up a company on the Internet is virtually cost-free!*

What is more, the same survey showed that, despite all the hype about Internet skills being very scarce, the same organisations thought they had experienced few problems caused by any lack of

> **KEY CONCEPT**
>
> Extending into e-commerce may be almost cost-free.

skills. In practice, the skills seem to be very simple to develop. That was the whole principle of the web; it was intended to be user-friendly.

On the other hand, it has to be recognised that an even greater majority of these organisations have not made a very professional job of their Internet start-up operations. And maybe that does reflect a lack of skill – not a lack of technical skills but of relevant business skills! I hope that this book will help to rectify at least part of that skills shortage.

E-retail product decisions

Once more extending the model of e-retail as a guide to likely developments in other sectors, in many respects the product decisions for e-retail are very similar to those for conventional retail. With the exception of the specialised knowledge services, what is being offered to the end user will not be too different. On the other hand, there are some factors which do change quite considerably.

As indicated above, the physical product or service probably won't change that much, but what may change is the degree of branding needed, since people will no longer be able to pick the product up and weigh it in their hand, or cast an eye over the staff who are about to deliver the service.

Hence there will have to be significant investment in building trust in a product which users must buy totally *unseen*.

Range

The breadth of the range of products and services available is where, at least in theory, the major benefit of e-commerce may lie. In theory, companies can offer enormous ranges

> **KEY CONCEPT**
>
> E-commerce can offer much wider ranges.

of goods, and even Wal-Mart in the US offers two or three times as many items on its website as it does in its largest superstore. What is more, this range can be extended almost indefinitely by linking to other vendors' websites, so you don't even have to stock the product. On the other hand, as we have seen with Amazon, that may pose problems where those other suppliers aren't set up to handle the logistics of selling to individual consumers. But, even so, it is an interesting challenge – and one, incidentally, which poses problems in helping your customers navigate through such a vast number of products. Once more, if they can't find a product they can't buy it!

Place

The traditional cry of the retailers, before the out-of-town stores took over, was 'location, location, location'. Their volume of trade depended upon *where* they were located on the

> **KEY CONCEPT**
>
> Website (process) design is crucial.

high street. In many situations, being just a few hundred yards further along the high street meant the difference between being the leading store and disaster. Clearly this is not the case with e-commerce. You can be sited anywhere in the world and still be accessible through the Internet. But, in a rather perverse way, similar rules apply – where 'location' here is the website. It's all about making certain your website is well placed, by building links with (and alliances with) the main search engines and portals, for example. It is also about the equivalent of having the best store front, with website design becoming increasingly important.

Promotion

It is becoming increasingly difficult to attract people to websites. They can't stroll along a virtual high street looking in windows: even using search engines may throw up hundreds of thousands of different store fronts to choose from. So promotion becomes even more important. Paradoxically, this is still by traditional means. Advertising agencies made a fortune out of the e-commerce start-ups, not least in selling – of all things – posters on the sides of buses! One leading agency said that the e-commerce boom had been the best wheeze ever for transferring funds from banks (who were funding the start-ups) to advertising agencies! But companies had to get their names known, which is one reason why the existing clicks and mortar retailers are much better placed – their names are already known. It is also why so much emphasis was placed by the new start-ups on their website addresses, so that customers could actually find them. Unfortunately, in the process, some start-ups forgot to mention what their offering was. As a potential customer, you might have known the name of the website, but you often hadn't got the vaguest idea what it offered!

Merchandising

One of the most important departments in traditional retail, especially department stores (which equate most closely to the new e-commerce operations) was that of merchandising. In essence, this was all about making it easy for your customer to find products in the store, making products attractive, so that customers would be attracted to them. The customer doesn't actually walk through the website – but once more website design is all-important.

 Vital questions and answers

- How has the move to e-commerce affected your strategies in terms of:
    - The range(s) of products/services you offer?
    - Where you sell and/or deliver these?
    - How you promote them?
    - How you merchandise them within your web-site(s)?

Databases

An essential part of one-to-one marketing is the establishment of a database. Usually – for medium to large organisations – it has to be a very sophisticated database (simply because of its size). I don't intend to go into all the technical details of databases in this book; as I said earlier, my advice is to get yourself the best experts to handle that. It's a very sophisticated subject, and one that you must get right – otherwise your database of members or customers will be of little use to you and may also alienate the very people you are trying to attract if you try to mail them with the wrong offer.

 **GETTING STARTED**

On the other hand, it is worth noting that there are several levels of sophistication, or stages of development, which can be seen in the use of databases:

> **KEY CONCEPT**
>
> Successful e-commerce often is directly related to effective database management.

1 *Sales database* – this is simply a list of customers, to be used by the sales department as part of its sales campaigns. It can range from customer address details, to be used perhaps in mailings, through to sophisticated reports of contacts with customers, their likes and dislikes, their order and sales ledger details, etc. In fact, even these extensions begin to introduce complexities because there will typically be several databases involved even here. For instance, the raw customer details will need to be merged on the customer file with financial transaction data held on the company's sales ledger.

2 *Range of databases* – in the second phase the company has a range of databases for different uses, organised by sales territories, by types of product, by different distribution operations, etc. Merging these together, or at least merging access to them (which is more likely) requires sophisticated database handling.

3 *Customer-focused databases* – instead of merging a number of company-oriented (and often product-based) databases, there is just one central customer-focused database which contains all information.

4 *True integration* – in this case the company has gone for what is often called the data warehouse, with one database design covering all its activities and allowing information to be pulled from every part of the business, to be accessed by everyone across the business.

5 *Extranet* – now, with the Internet (and particularly with EDI) it is even possible to share databases – especially those relating to purchasing – across a range of organisations. This level of sophistication may well be beyond all but the very large organisations, but they can use it to great effect to improve their efficiency.

Vital questions and answers

■ Which of these stages is your own organisation at?

Manipulating data

The core theory of direct marketing, whether through e-commerce or some other medium, is remarkably simple – it is merely a matter of matching the requisite marketing approach to the individual. This is a philosophy which should be even more effective in e-marketing. As we have seen, though, problems arise handling the vast amounts of data involved. Some solutions to this may be:

- *Expert systems* – the longer-term solution may be to teach computers to make the necessary decisions. This is currently being explored by some of developers, such as Computer Associates, who produce the software for very large databases.
- *Simplified approaches* – in the shorter term it may be easier to handle decisions at an aggregate level, going back to what clustering does for market research results. You apply the decisions to groups of people who look the same; in other words, you use a form of segmentation.
- *Simple decisions* – alternatively, you can match the overall purchasing profile of a customer and make promotional

offers based on this, which is what supermarkets have done with their own loyalty cards.

Direct marketing

This is the model which probably gives us the greatest insight into how one-to-one marketing through the Internet can be used. It offers some of the best examples of successful practice in e-retail for today's markets. On the other hand, so far the best examples are not necessarily about e-commerce, but about direct mail operations – such as GUS (Great Universal Stores) in the UK.

The most general examples of such direct marketing are the *mail-order* catalogues we have already talked about, put out by organisations such as Littlewoods and Grattan in the UK and as early as 1887 by Sears Roebuck in the US. These are, in effect, department stores by mail. The core cost justification is that they don't have to take large amounts of very expensive floor-space on the high street. On the other hand, they may still have substantial overheads in terms of getting their catalogues to customers and fulfilling orders by post.

> **KEY CONCEPT**
>
> Direct marketing experience may hold some of the most important lessons for e-commerce.

If we want to look at the ideal, in terms of selling, it must still be the one-to-one, face-to-face, meeting between the customer and an expert salesperson. This allows the fullest possible interaction, to establish exactly what the customer needs are, although such excellent sales personnel are rare indeed! This is, however, only viable when the value of the sale can justify the cost of that face-to-face interaction, which may run to several hundred pounds for one call if all the overheads are included. This means that some form of intermediary has to be used, usually a retailer for consumer sales or a distributor with business-to-business.

Using electronic links, such as the Internet and web, in effect creates a new form of intermediary. As we have seen, because it may replace an existing range of intermediaries this has recently been called disintermediation.

Electronic catalogues

Of course the big difference between printed catalogues and those over the Internet or the web is how they are accessed. You flick through printed catalogues, sometimes using the index at the back until you find what you want. In the electronic approach in general, you can only go through some form of menu or index. This makes browsing much more difficult, but on the other hand makes access to specific products easier – as long as a good index or word search facility is available. The key factor, as always, is how well designed the systems are.

> **KEY CONCEPT**
>
> Much of e-commerce is catalogue-based.

Mailings

The starting point for direct marketing has previously been direct mail. Until quite recently, this was the letter delivered by the postman. This was, generally speaking, remarkably efficient and, as the sophistication of databases grew, so the letter could be highly personalised – and accordingly it became ever more effective. In this context, the use of e-mail (the level of usage of which is not currently very high, outside industrial markets) adds very little – it is just a different form of letter.

Whichever form is used, it does offer precise targeting and personalisation, which is very important in building a simulated face-to-face relationship with the consumer. Research indicates that simply by putting your customer's name at the beginning of a letter you can increase response to any form of mail by a factor of two or three, and by personalising it further response increases by an order of magnitude.

Clubs

The greatest benefit of direct mail over advertising is likely to be that of continuity. Thus, you can build campaigns over a period of time, and in particular you can build your next letter on the basis of the response to

> **KEY CONCEPT**
>
> Relationships may be most productively developed through clubs.

the last one – this is tailoring at its most effective. In this way the supplier runs a continuity programme, of which the *club* is the best example. This extends the customer contact beyond the initial transaction, and in the process it progressively develops the relationship, steadily learning more about the customer so that future marketing may be more precise.

As I have already said, it is obvious that one of the key objectives of e-commerce vendors should be to build loyalty. In this context, probably the best model therefore is that of the clubs developed by the vendors who specialised in the previous direct marketing by mail. The way such clubs are built is by one-to-one contact, with tailored letters sent out on a regular basis. It is not through financial incentives. On the other hand, the loyalty points systems run by a number of retail stores may also be applicable. Yahoo! already runs something like that, although it does it rather badly, not even making it clear to the people receiving the loyalty points what they can do with them!

Personal data profiles

I have already said that normal market research, surveying *groups* of consumers, does not work as easily over the

Internet. On the other hand, by making use of the one-to-one relationship which can be established this way, there is no need for such group research, since the information which can be gathered (on the basis of day-to-day contact perhaps) is about *each* individual customer. This material, because it is very specific, is much more powerful – just as long as you can make productive use of it. Again, this is where databases are crucial, and dealing with the complexities of databases once more becomes the central skill which needs to be developed.

Data collection

Thus, the greatest value comes from knowing about the individual customer, something mass marketers can never do. With e-commerce you really can follow the purchasing behaviour of each individual, better target them, and as a result you can tailor your product or service to exactly meet their needs. This can provide an incredibly powerful advantage, if you make use of it. On the other hand, in collecting this information, you have to be very sensitive about the questions you ask of the individual. Accordingly, you have to balance the knowledge you want against how they may react to some of the more sensitive questions.

Some personal data can, however, be collected by existing methods, such as EPOS and EFTPOS. This information on conventional buying habits can be collected as part of a visit to a local supermarket. There are also organisations that amalgamate other people's databases to build pictures of individual customers – and these can be bought commercially.

But, at the end of the day, by far the most important database you can have is the one which you create in-house – even though many organisations neglect this. It can be an extremely valuable resource, sometimes the most valuable of all. Not long ago I talked with the corporate planning group of one of the large high street banks, who were asking themselves whether they really were in the business of money or in that of database organisation, because they had come to recognise that the main value of the company was in its knowledge of its customers.

 PAUSE FOR THOUGHT

- Which of these direct marketing approaches does your organisation use, and which does it find most effective?
  - Direct marketing in general
  - Electronic catalogues
  - (Postal) mailings
  - E-mailings
  - Continuity programmes
  - Clubs
  - Personalisation
  - Personal data profiles
  - Customer databases

Direct advertising

Having looked at how direct marketing can be used to sell and distribute products direct to the customer, direct advertising (using mail or e-mail), as opposed to mass media advertising, is just one part of the overall picture. But it can make an especially important contribution to targeted precision marketing campaigns, especially those in the industrial sector. It is one way, for example, of generating large numbers of prospects which can then be followed up by face-to-face calls.

Normal postal mail response rates may be around 1 to 2%, or even lower. As yet no equivalent figures have been produced for e-mail – but there's no reason to expect them to be any higher. Indeed, because of people's fear of opening strange e-mails (and especially their attachments, which may contain viruses), the figure may be much lower. Even though I have professionally maintained anti-virus protection, at a very high level, I will not open an e-mail these days unless I know exactly where it's from.

The advantages of direct e-mail

Even so, e-mail does demonstrate certain benefits:

> **KEY CONCEPT**
>
> Direct e-mail advertising can be targeted and personalised.

- *Specific targeting* – by far the most important advantage is being able to target individual customers.
- *Personalisation* – closely tied to this is the ability to *personalise* the message you send to the customer. This is the nearest you can get to having a salesperson call on customers in a mass market.
- *Optimisation* – because you can progressively converse with an individual, you can gradually learn which marketing approaches are most effective with that individual – or perhaps with a similar group of individuals.
- *Accumulation* – your information about the customer *accumulates* over time as you gain more and more responses from them.
- *Flexibility* – finally, the campaigns may be mounted very quickly, or changed almost at a moment's notice.

Vital questions and answers

■ Which of these might be most important to your own
e-commerce operations?

On the other hand there are some downsides:

■ *Cost* – in conventional mail campaigns it is inevitable that
the cost per thousand of traditional (postal) direct mail
will be higher than for the mass media. On the other
hand, since many of the costs (from electronic processing
through to the actual cost of sending the e-mail), may be
much lower for electronic direct mail, the cost penalty
may not be so high. *Indeed, the significantly lower costs
(against postal delivery) may eventually be the main reason for
the development of this form of direct marketing.*

■ *Poor-quality lists* – even in direct postal mail, where there
is a long history of companies building lists of target
individuals, the quality of these lists has often been poor,
and they often required a lot of cleaning to get rid of
duplication. Where such lists don't even exist on e-mail,
this may be a major drawback, postponing developments
for some time to come!

■ *Relative lack of development* – direct mail practices have
long been the Cinderella of mass marketing techniques.
The only lessons learned were learned from practical
experience – though in fact they may have been no worse
for that. More importantly, very few lessons indeed have
(yet) been learned about e-mail.

Vital questions and answers

■ Which of these might pose the most problems for
your own operations?

Mail lists

Whatever the form you choose, however, the first starting point must be a *list* of people that you are going to contact. This is very difficult to obtain for e-mail, and once more the suggestion is that your own customer list, and list of the other contacts (such as enquirers) that you have made, is probably the best starting point. It is almost certainly the clearest starting point. Hence it is clearly important that you invest in your own database. If nothing else, this should mean that anyone contacting your organisation, for whatever reason, should be put on that database. Most organisations' databases only contain the details of people who have fought their way through the various stages of the purchasing process to become customers. All the other prospects, who have identified themselves by inquiring about the product, are typically discarded. This means that you have very little idea what the success rate is in converting these prospects to customer – but in the context of direct mail it also means that these valuable prospects are not even kept in your sights!

A particularly effective form of mailing list, usually generated from a website, can be created if you simply ask the people visiting the site if they wish to be put on your mailing list. You may have to give them some incentive, such as making news items available to them, but once you have got their attention – and their permission (covered earlier as 'permission marketing') – they provide a particularly valuable form of mailing list.

 Vital questions and answers

- What lists (in-house or commercial) do you have at your disposal?
- How complete and valuable are these?

Direct offers

Unlike most general media advertising, where a whole range of factors can be brought into play even in a 30-second commercial, the direct mail (especially the direct e-mail) offer has to be very simple and very clear.

I've already made this point about websites. Electronic communications require that you simplify everything to their basics. This is especially true of an e-mail campaign. Remember that you have to get to the prospect with

> **KEY CONCEPT**
>
> An e-mail offer has to be short, simple and very clear.

the *subject line* of an e-mail, otherwise there is a very good chance they won't even open it. You have to recognise that the e-mail may arrive in their mailbox at the same time as a dozen junk e-mails. Accordingly, it has to attract the recipient's attention away from those before you can even get them to look at it!

Letters

The greatest amount of mythology in traditional direct mail revolved around what was the most effective form of letter. There were some fascinating variations. Thus, some people insisted that a short letter was essential, and others that thought a long letter was more effective.

My own experience is that, once again, it's horses for courses and the content of the letter has to be set by the information you need to convey. Thus, if you have a very simple message, keep it to two or three lines, which is all that is needed. On the other hand, if you have a substantial technical announcement then you must make it as long as necessary. As long as the information is useful and interesting to the target audience, they will read it.

Having said all that, this choice only really applies to *postal* letters. The dynamics are such that *all e-mails must be short.* Remember you can always put a web return address on the letter, to which the recipient can hyperlink, so that you can expand further if you do manage to whet their appetite.

Thereafter, the best advice is *keep it simple*! The other, returning to the first theme above, is that the subject line, the one that they will see on their e-mail system, is worth all the rest of the e-mail put together.

> **KEY CONCEPT**
>
> The core of the e-mail message must be short, and summarised in the subject line of the message.

In postal mail there is also a whole industry devoted to designing inserts! Something similar may develop with e-mails when more use web software to 'design' the content. If you have ever opened some of the club mailings, for example from Reader's Digest, you may have had difficulty appreciating what the real message was about because in such mailings, there are so many free offers, hidden under instructions to 'tick this box', 'stick that stamp' etc. It is arguable that – for most consumers – such confusion adds nothing to the mailing. But presumably the Reader's Digest management knows what motivates their own particular audience.

In terms of e-mails, there is only one piece of advice, and that is simple. *Don't send any attachments*! With so many viruses floating around, it is asking too much of people to expect them to open your attachment before they get the main part of the message.

> **KEY CONCEPT**
>
> Don't use e-mail attachments, but hot-link to a website.

Instead, direct them to a website, by providing a hyperlink, where – assuming their software is effective – they don't have to worry about corrupting their system.

In the good old days the key element, which 'closed' the sale, was the reply-paid card – so that all a customer had to do was fill it in and send it back. Even then the response rates were much higher if these were already personalised (with the recipient's individual name and address), so that all they had to do was tick a box and put the card in the mail. Of course, the e-mail equivalent is much easier. All the recipients have to do is reply – maybe by doing nothing more than hitting the Reply button. You then know everything you need to know about them, at least to start a conversation with them.

 PAUSE FOR THOUGHT

- A useful exercise at this stage is to look at some of your own recent mailings, if possible in comparison with some from your competitors (or, failing that, from those published as winners of industry-wide awards).
- How does your work rate against these benchmarks?

Response rate measurement

The great advantage of direct mail is that you can judge the effectiveness of *each* mailing. This means that you can try out all sorts of different approaches, and very easily see which one works best. The classic approach to this task, incidentally, in mass media is to get the customer to write back to department XXX – the department number tells you which particular advertisement they are responding to, and hence the effectiveness of that particular journal/magazine and/or your message in it. Similarly you can get the same information built into your e-mail campaigns, so when respondents reply you can get as much information as you want. The end result is that you can learn from every campaign that you use.

How do you make money?

CHAPTER 10

Overview

One of the biggest questions facing the new knowledge industries in general, and e-commerce in particular, is how do you get value out – for your shareholders – on an operational basis. With physical products, on which neoclassical economics is based, you can reach out and touch them – and see how value is added as they go through the factory. This doesn't happen with e-commerce services. In particular, if you look at the concept of diminishing returns, economic theory assumes there is a scarcity of product and that each extra unit costs more to make. Unfortunately for economists, in the case of knowledge, the more you use it the more valuable it becomes. This is a conundrum that economists have yet to grasp. More problematically, while you can see the value to the individual of being able to talk with other people around the world by e-mail, it is not immediately obvious how that personal value is released in economic or commercial terms.

The objective of this chapter is to look at a few of the options available.

Reverting to the major theme of this book, e-commerce can often be seen as one channel – albeit

CONTINUED . . . **Overview**

one covering promotion as well as distribution –
amongst a range of channels. Hence channel management, and balancing these channels against each other,
becomes an important function. This chapter suggests a
few ways this might be managed.

- Portal revenues
- Advertisement sales
- Content sales
- Banner advertising
- Sponsorship
- Traffic figures
- Channel management
- Affiliate programmes
- Vertical marketing
- Distribution logistics

Portal revenues and earnings

The portals are desperately trying to find some way of
releasing the value of their members. On the back of the
initial concept, some of them managed to persuade the
financial markets they had value – though this is now much
less than it was when the dot.com boom pushed their value
out of all proportion – but they haven't yet found a way of
doing it on an *operational basis*.

Almost all, with the possible
exception of AOL, are still making
losses.

According to Forrester
Research, in 2000 only 23% of US

KEY CONCEPT

It is very difficult to release
operational earnings from
most e-commerce activities.

sites were profitable! Sites tried in the first instance to skim off the discount the line rental companies offered them, but that was soon undercut when competitors passed this on to their customers. Now they claim that they can make money by advertising – although the same research pointed out that there was too much free content for even this to work!

 PAUSE FOR THOUGHT

■ To the best of your knowledge, what revenues and earnings (at the net contribution level, if not net profit) does your e-commerce earn?

  ■ Revenue £ . . . . . .
  ■ Net contribution £ . . . . . .

Selling content

The ultimate solution must be that customers pay for content; and Microsoft, in terms of its MSN portal, is already planning to apply such usage charges to fund new development. Unfortunately, according to Forrester, less than 10% of current customers plan to pay for any sort of content. Even among the 26% who had at some time already paid for content, less than half said they would pay again! They are too used to getting it for free. E-markets have a long way to go before they can stand on their own feet – which, once again, is where the $e^+marketing$ (clicks and mortar) vendors, with their existing revenue base and their ability to extend their existing profit-making activities – have the edge.

Discounts and *royalties* may ultimately be the salvation of such portals. In this case, when the customer comes to a vendor through one of these portals the vendor gives a royalty to the portal – in much the same way as a supplier rewards retailers for stocking their goods. In this way Amazon, for example, makes a nice living from the trade discounts it receives on its books (but not, as yet, on much else it sells!).

> **KEY CONCEPT**
>
> Making money out of the content, by royalty or commission, may be the most important source of income in the longer term.

 PAUSE FOR THOUGHT

- What content do you have which is saleable?
- What discounts and commissions might you be able to earn?

Selling advertisements

As hinted above, you will have seen how many websites are plastered with advertisements. The downside of this is that it is often difficult for a customer to find any *information*, which presumably was their reason for visiting the site!

Paradoxically, there still doesn't seem to be much demand for advertising space on these sites; the rumour is that most of these ads are given away free as part of package deals with other advertising media, although US figures suggest that,

> **KEY CONCEPT**
>
> Advertising is a major, but currently unprofitable, source of revenue.

there at least, this new medium might soon be worth several billion dollars per annum. Forrester Research has predicted that online advertising will increase to be worth $40 billion by 2005! On the other hand, adverts get in the way of what the customer wants from websites. One description, which I like, is 'interruption marketing' – they just get in the way of the real business. Whatever you think of them, as yet only a very few sites make money out of banner ads.

Even though it is not offering much of a challenge to the domination of the existing mass media, it is claimed that online advertising has a number of advantages over traditional mass media advertising:

> **KEY CONCEPT**
>
> Web advertising should be more targetable than mass media, though its greatest advantage should be its opportunities for interaction.

- *Targetability* – with one-to-one marketing, and very tightly defined groups, you should be able to offer exactly what the advertiser wants in terms of target audience.
- *Tracking* – the impact on these customers can be tracked, and the advertising messages optimised.
- *Deliverability and flexibility* – the ad is available all the time, not just when you see it in the dentist's waiting room, for example. Furthermore, a campaign can be launched, updated or cancelled immediately.
- *Interactivity* – the customer can interact with the product. When they see your advertisement they can click on it and be taken to your website where considerably more information can be provided to them. This is probably the major advantage, not least because the very limited capacity banners on the original website can carry very little information.

 PAUSE FOR THOUGHT

■ Which of these can you offer, in terms of your website(s), to potential advertisers?

Banner advertising

A whole range of different banner sizes are available on sites: 468 × 60 pixels is a 'full banner', while 88 × 31 pixels is a 'micro-button'.

You only have to go to a typical website to see the complexity of the different advertising patterns you can use. This may mean something to advertisers, but it probably just means a mess to most

viewers! Within these advertisements, though, there are all sorts of other things you can do. At first, bright colours were used, now animation is more popular, though if it's too complicated it may take so long to download that the viewer has moved on before anything happens.

Some suggestions of techniques you can use to enhance the impact of adverts are:

- *Simplicity* – as I have already said these are more like posters; they can't handle much detail and you should use no more than seven words (and make certain these load very fast indeed) and always use bright colours and limited animation to attract attention.
- *Buttons* – providing a button within your advertisement, so that viewers can click through to your website to get more information, is one of the positive features of advertising on the web.
- *Following* – sometimes, if you're very clever, you can follow the customer as they browse through websites, though you should beware of harassing them – they will hate you for this.
- *Rich media banners* – these are a variation which allow you to complete the whole transaction within the banner. This means that the customer doesn't have to go off to another website and trawl through that. Instead, as long as you

can fit it within seven words, you can close your sale there and then.

PAUSE FOR THOUGHT

- How does your own site(s) measure up against these?

Sponsorship

One subtle form of advertising is, as with other media, sponsoring the part of the site the customer is visiting. This enables you to take away a great deal of the aggravation that they find from having sites cluttered with advertisements, and it can look something like editorial – which is always more influential. On the other hand, be careful that you don't do so much of it that you degrade the real editorial.

Another variation is that you can place your advertisement only with the customers who are looking for the specific features which your product can provide. At other times, they see different advertisements.

In theory, at least, it is also possible to insert ads – called *interstitials* – while the web page is loading, but these have fallen out of favour, quite justifiably. Viewers hate waiting for sites to download and feel that the ads they are seeing, while waiting for the real content, get in the way – and those ads are penalised as a result!

Traffic figures

One of the greatest advantages of the web should be that you can get reports of traffic through your ad, at various levels from the number of people visiting your website down to the numbers simply passing through individual pages and ads:

■ *Hits* – website owners typically judge the success of their site by the number of hits or visits it receives, but this is the most basic measure and can deceive. You may be counting as a full hit every graphic which the page calls up to create the picture. In addition, some visitors to your site may actually be search-engine spiders cataloguing sites.

■ *Page views* – this simplifies the picture somewhat by simply measuring how many complete pages are viewed. This is almost as widely used as the hit measure.

■ *Caching* – a separate problem is under-counting. When a page is called from a popular site it may be cached on the user's local server (often called a 'proxy server') and any further users coming soon afterwards will be given this cached page, without getting near the main site, and thus not being counted by the main site.

Researched traffic measures

In the same way that other media, both television and press, have their audience figures measured, this can be done for websites:

◆ *Circulation* – the hit and page figures are audited by a central body, such as ABC or Nielsen, as for other media.

◆ *Readership* – a panel of users is researched, although you should be aware that population, and hence the sampling frames, are currently suspect.

Impressions

One classic device for charging advertising space, which is also used for television spots, is that of paying by impressions: the number of people seeing your ad. But sometimes you can do a deal whereby the site owner only charges for the visitors who actually make *click-throughs* to your site; but you should be certain these are worthwhile visitors. Occasionally you can pay for *leads*, for only those who visit your site and fill in a form – though understandably site owners are less keen on this sort of approach.

Channel management

If we go back to management theory, many of the theoretical considerations before the advent of e-commerce revolved around the cost of the channel. On the other hand, many of the practical considerations revolved around the *control* of these channels. Away from the Internet, the small company usually has no alternative but to use intermediaries, often several layers of them, since that is the only way that they can distribute their product or service away from a local area. On the other hand, large companies have the choice of a wide range of delivery methods.

Whatever the environment, however, the first level of management control is choosing the organisations which will become the key parts of your channel structure. Clearly the central organisation itself has some control over this choice, though not always. At one extreme, in mass consumer goods markets, where the only requirement is a logistical one – getting the product or service to the widest cross-section of the public – the main concern is typically to maximise ultimate distribution. At the other extreme, where there are very sophisticated technical products or those which have a distinct luxury image, the supplier may be much more concerned about managing quality control in a small number of outlets. Much the same range of decisions have to be taken in e-commerce. The Application Service Provider (ASP) or portal, which is subcontracted to provide part or the whole of the service, is especially important.

Affiliate programmes

Perhaps the most important approach, which has emerged with the Internet, is that of affiliation. Thus, organisations try to find partners with similar interests who will help to drive total revenues.

For example, Amazon is supposed to obtain more than 10% of its revenue from its affiliate programmes – and it has more than 100,000 affiliate sites linked to its

> **KEY CONCEPT**
>
> Affiliates are a productive way of sharing costs.

own site and selling its products. The exact form of affiliation can vary. Products may be co-branded, or presented as house brands, or the vendor may bypass existing members of the chain by disintermediating them rather than integrating them. The important point is that the host vendor provides the services that the affiliate typically can't afford to run, and in return sales by the latter improve the overall throughput of the former.

Vertical channels

One relatively recent development integrates the channel across the original supplier and all the other members of the distribution chain, working through to retailers where

> **KEY CONCEPT**
>
> E-commerce allows vertical channels to be productive.

they are needed. The result is a unified system. This can come about because one member owns all the others – corporate systems integration. This is a logical move for Internet service providers. Thus airlines now sell seats directly over the Internet, in competition with high street travel shops.

Another approach is that of contractual systems, where one prominent member of the distribution chain uses its strength to manage other members' activities. This has traditionally been led by manufacturers, but with the Internet it is more likely that the portals, such as AOL, will enforce this type of arrangement.

The purpose of vertical channels is to enhance control over the distribution chain, in the process removing some of the uncertainties of trading. It is a strategy which is typically best pursued at the mature stage in the market, since at earlier stages it may even reduce profits. It is also arguable that it diverts attention from the real business at hand. Both of these suggest that it is probably too early for it to become a major factor in e-commerce.

The terminology can be confusing, for vertical portals are not the same as vertical channels. Instead, they're more like speciality shops which have taken over most of the high street now that the superstores have migrated to out-of-town sites. Each of these speciality stores focuses on a range of products; typically books have been featured in bookstores and now are featured on the vertical portal Amazon. As we saw earlier, of course, horizontal portals aim to be everything to everyone – a one-stop shop, such as AOL is looking to be.

 PAUSE FOR THOUGHT

- What would affiliate programmes, or vertical channels, do for your e-commerce operations?

Distribution logistics

Considering the intangible nature of e-commerce, it may seem silly to be talking about the problems of shipping physical goods. This is included here, though, quite simply because this has often been the most difficult problem faced by organisations moving into e-commerce. Even the clicks and mortar vendors, those with existing businesses which might be expected to have good distribution set-ups, have found that the problem of shipping small parcels to individual consumers is very different to their normal business model. Many of the new start-ups, on the other hand, have trusted themselves to carriers who developed their reputation before e-commerce came along. It was for this reason that Amazon had to spend so much money in creating its own distribution network – since fulfilment, actually getting the product to the consumer, is just as important as having an effective website. It is particularly true that, because it takes a short time to place an order on a website, people seem to expect the product to arrive at the front door almost as quickly. Some organisations, most notably Amazon, do promise delivery within a day or two if the book ordered is in stock. Unfortunately, most organisations cannot promise delivery within a week or two, and that invalidates many of benefits of e-commerce.

Virtual businesses

As a footnote to this section, one of the great hopes for the e-commerce revolution was that it would free businesses to do what they were best at. Thus, the separate elements were to be subcontracted to specialists in the field: production of the product put out to a manufacturing facility, advertising to an agency, distribution to a carrier. The reality has proved to be rather different. The idea that a small handful of people sitting in a central head office could use the Internet to manipulate a vast virtual business empire has proved much more difficult in practice.

Business-to-business (B2B)

CHAPTER 11

Overview

One rather different area of e-commerce is that of business-to-business (B2B). This, in the short term at least, will be much bigger than all the other parts of e-commerce. Even so, many of the communications elements parallel the B2C activities which we have already covered in detail. In terms of the specific B2B elements, which revolve around operations management as much as the Internet, the objectives are to:

Explore the operations management activities which lie behind EDI (Electronic Data Interchange), the method used to integrate operations across different corporations; list the benefits of EDI, especially of Internet-based EDI; and explore the new electronic marketplaces which are emerging.

- Business-to-Employee (B2E) and peer-to-peer
- Electronic Data Interchange (EDI)
- Operations management
- Material Requirements Planning (MRP)
- Just In Time (JIT)
- Make or buy
- Limitations of EDI

CONTINUED . . . Overview

- EDI on the Internet
- Business exchanges
- B2B Internet
- E-commerce marketplaces
- Supplier-oriented marketplaces
- Intermediary-oriented marketplaces
- Buyer-oriented marketplaces
- Virtual corporations

B2B markets

In general the markets in this sector are different to business-to-consumer B2C) markets for a number of reasons:

1 They are more *complex*. The typical consumer purchase will be a single item bought by a single person from one organisation. A typical operation in business-to-business is for an assembly, of a range of purchases from different suppliers and managed by a range of people. Managers need to understand all the relationships involved before they can manage the operation itself. Under all of this complexity has to be the much more rigorous form of customer relationship management needed.

2 The *relationships* involved can be much more complex. We have already looked at the complex sale, and this is indicative of the wide range of people involved. But the whole relationship goes much wider, across the many people also involved in the day-to-day operations.

3 *Customer relationship management* also has to go much further, where the operations of both organisations

depend upon the relationship between them. *Trust* is also even more important, and needs to be based on each side learning how the other side operates.

4 The key parameter offered is not that of price, despite what many would claim, but *performance*. With such a complex web of products and services, and the relationships between the organisations involved, the performance of every part of this is crucial, since breakdown in one part can destroy the whole. This is particularly true in terms of timeliness of performance. It is crucial that each partner delivers their offering at the time when it is needed – if it is a week late then everything else is at least a week late.

 PAUSE FOR THOUGHT

- Which of these factors apply to your own B2B relationships?
- What are the implications of these for how you may do business with your suppliers, and possibly some customers as well?

The key point to note is the *interrelationship* of all the various operations.

Business-to-employee (B2E) and peer-to-peer

Business-to-business is split into a number of different sectors. Some of the sectors are very like, and parallel, those of business-to-consumer. There is also a new sector called *business-to-employee* (B2E),

> **KEY CONCEPT**
>
> B2E and peer-to-peer follow much the same rules as for B2C.

which revolves around management's communication with their employees or, depending upon your interpretation, outside vendors selling direct to the key personnel in their customer organisations.

Equally, there is peer-to-peer. In the form of communications across intranets, within companies, this probably already accounts for most of the communication involved in electronic marketplaces. Although, as we have seen, this is mainly in the form of e-mail, it has considerably enhanced internal productivity. It has not got rid of paper (in fact it seems to generate ever more paper) but it does mean that more and more people are better and better informed as to what is going on in their organisation. I don't intend to expand either of these further here: the relevant points have already been covered by my descriptions of the other elements of e-commerce.

EDI (Electronic Data Interchange)

At the other extreme, in large organisations, there is already extensive use of electronic communications to integrate operational activities. This is very effective, but also very complex. It is the province of EDI – Electronic Data Interchange. The advent of the Internet has simply extended the range of channels that are available for this type of communication.

EDI is a means of standardising communications between organisations, specifically in terms of the standard documentation they transmit to each other. It covers routine business documents which are transmitted over secure telephone links (or extranet). Typically it involves orders,

> **KEY CONCEPT**
>
> Use of EDI is complex, but concerns operations management rather than ICT.

invoices, payments and delivery information – operations at the heart of the purchasing procedures which exist between bilateral organisations. These are translated into a standard format which can be understood by computers in each organisation. It means that nobody has to interface these communications, to change the data to make it suitable for use by their own computer systems. As soon as one of the parties issues new documentation it is incorporated in their partners' systems.

EDI predates e-commerce by several decades. It is arguable that it has been around, in a variety of forms, for up to 30 years. Its development parallels not so much that of the Internet but that of computerised stock and production control systems.

 PAUSE FOR THOUGHT

- Do you deploy classical EDI? (If the answer is yes you will probably want to skip much of the rest of this chapter, since it is likely that you *already* know more than the content here offers!)

Operations management

If you have not yet been exposed to EDI, it is worth looking at some of the complexities of operations management, since it is this, rather than ICT, which will determine how or even whether you use EDI.

At the most basic level, methods of inventory control vary in sophistication from the simplest of manual systems through to the most complex of computerised systems. EDI operates at the latter end of this spectrum.

One of the simplest, and most effective, methods is to have two 'bins' of a product (or service). When the first 'bin' is empty it is replaced by the second, full one; and another bin of product is put on order. If the requirements of such a 'component' represent a very small part of the overall cost, this approach may be the easiest to implement, and may well be the most effective. It is the area where, perhaps, the new 'exchanges' (or catalogue suppliers) may work well.

A rather more sophisticated version of this simple system, which (as the 'Kanban' system) has been very effectively used by Japanese manufacturers, is to provide a card with each 'bin' supplied. When the bin is empty the card is returned, and automatically generates an order on the supplier.

The traditional standby, before computers came along, was to have a card for each product, though, unlike the 'Kanban' system, these were usually held centrally, by the purchasing or inventory control departments. Each stock movement was duly recorded on one of the relevant product/ component cards (in, as goods were received from the supplier, and out, as goods were despatched to the customer), and the resulting balance adjusted.

These have now been replaced, almost universally, by computer-based equivalents. The term 'stock control' used for these is, incidentally, usually a misnomer, since in most cases it is in reality only stock recording. As with the card systems, it merely states (based on the movements in and out) the balance of stock. In the more sophisticated versions it will also allow for on-order and back-order items. All of these are records of what has happened. The stock control, the decision of when and what amount to reorder, is the responsibility of the humans using the information, but the computer may help with this by providing a reminder when the stock falls below the minimum or reorder point, and may also provide assistance with some of the calculations such as Economic Order Quantities (EOQ).

In the service industries it usually also shows the 'slots' (usually time-based, even in terms of theatre bookings) available at some time in the future. Something like this lies at the heart of the operations control systems of most organisations. You can start to see why EDI may be a step too far for these!

Materials requirements planning (MRP)

The most sophisticated computerised systems are those which track all the components of the product or service (possibly running into hundreds in number),

> **KEY CONCEPT**
>
> The heart of EDI operations may be MRP.

which come together to make a technologically sophisticated product or service, where the demand of these components is 'dependent' (that is, the decision to make one assembly, say, automatically generates a demand for a range of components, each in different volumes).

The starting point for such systems is usually a *Bill of Material Processor* (BOMP) package, which is a tree-structured database recording what components go into each sub-assembly, which in turn goes into ever larger assemblies that make up the final product – whether this is a food mixer, or a 747 airliner, or a financial services offering. It will show, for example, that the final product such as a washing machine uses 25 screws of a particular type: 10 in the drum assembly, 4 in the timer sub-assembly and 11 in the final assembly process.

MRP also allows for the time taken at each level of assembly, thus offsetting the orders for each 'kit' of parts. In this way, it will also know the starting dates of each of the preceding operations for a product to be delivered on a certain date, and this is the basis of its 'master schedule' (together with the 'planned orders' for individual components) which ultimately leads to the output of that product. The advantage of MRP, in theory, is that work can be accurately scheduled so that there is no waiting between stages. Most other systems have large stocks of in-process inventory, which wait between the various stages until the kits of parts (and the machine and manpower resources) are available for the next stage. This increases inventory and also results in long, and unpredictable, lead-times. To be fully effective, in many larger organisations, EDI has to be able to handle such complexities – and its managers have to be skilled in MRP and beyond.

Just in time (JIT)

One development in inventory holding, pioneered by Toyota in the 1950s, is JIT. In this approach, components are delivered from the suppliers direct to the production

> **KEY CONCEPT**
>
> E-commerce can make good use of JIT.

line just as they are needed (or at least only a few hours before). Thus, almost no stocks are held by the manufacturer. It is, accordingly, a very efficient method of holding (or perhaps more accurately, not holding) inventory. In the case of the electronic services offered by many e-commerce operations, this may be even simpler to organise.

It does, however, have a number of hidden disadvantages for 'hard' physical products – especially those interfacing with other organisations through EDI – though perhaps not for 'soft' services. Of these the most important is its lack of flexibility. It demands 'flat scheduling', which means that the production runs must be forecast several weeks in advance, since the comparable production runs by the suppliers will take place some time in advance of the final assembly, and their plans must allow for this. Changes in plan are not possible in the short term – though, if the key components are produced in-house and flexible manufacturing (especially reduced set-up times) employed, this disadvantage may be minimised. Equally, the much vaunted inventory savings by the manufacturer may sometimes come about simply because the suppliers are holding buffer stocks instead.

One senior manager at Toyota said to me recently, 'JIT is straightforward, indeed easy, when you get everything working correctly. Mind you, it took us several decades to achieve this!' This was delivered as a joke, but contains a great deal of truth. It undoubtedly took Toyota many years, probably decades, to achieve the benefits they now gain from JIT. Those Western manufacturers trying to install JIT over a weekend may like to reflect on this fact!

EDI certainly promises great advances in JIT but, as the Toyota quote suggests, this may be a far from easy path to greater productivity!

Make or buy

In recent years, an important trend has been to buy in all those items which can be purchased elsewhere. Only those items which cannot be bought elsewhere, and hence represent the special expertise of the organisation, should (according to this new philosophy) be manufactured in-house. More realistically applied, the new approach compares the cost (preferably of all the factors – not just manufacturing costs) of producing in-house with that of buying-in, and places the business wherever it will be most efficiently handled. This is a hidden assumption behind much of EDI.

The following factors, it is suggested, should be taken into account in this decision:

- *Quality* – it may be that the quality produced by the outside

> **KEY CONCEPT**
>
> E-commerce offers greater opportunities for 'buy-in' as opposed to 'making'.

supplier is higher than that which could be produced in house; this should be true if a supplier specialises in this element of the product or service.

- *Capacity* – the need for outside supply may be forced by the lack of internal capacity. On the other hand, the organisation will need to be convinced that external supplies can be guaranteed, and will not be 'cornered' by competitors when industry-wide demand increases.
- *Labour* – the impact on the organisation's own staff (who are stakeholders too) may be critical.
- *Scheduling* – the degree of control (as well as the proximity) of in-house production allows a much faster response to crises. Conversely, the use of outside suppliers demands tighter control of supplier deliveries (as is the case with JIT) and more progress chasing – or higher inventories.
- *Skill* – the supplier may have greater skills available. On the other hand, any organisation would be foolish to contract out operations which are the key to its own competitive advantage.
- *Cost* – only when all the other factors have been satisfied does cost come into play (the reverse of what happens in most such decisions). Unfortunately, in practice, it is not easy to compare costs on a like for like basis.

 PAUSE FOR THOUGHT

- Which of these are most important in terms of your own make or buy decisions?

The basic make or buy decision is, therefore, a complex one. As a result, it is often taken on the basis of principle (or dogma) rather than clear facts.

The overall message is that EDI – which has to be based on much more than dogma – is a very specialised form of

B2B, and managing it is very complex so, before you get involved with it, you have some very serious planning to undertake!

Limitations of traditional EDI

Despite all these complications, EDI can make a tremendous impact on the way large organisations manage their business relationships. On the other hand, precisely because of these complications, it is currently used in less than 1% of all organisations. Communications may be standardised, but they are still very sophisticated – and the computer interfaces are even more sophisticated. Finally, operations management systems run by their computers are even more complicated.

For EDI to work, the two organisations involved must have a common set of standards concerning the electronic interchange of data. Thus, in parti-

> **KEY CONCEPT**
>
> True EDI is implemented by less than 1% of organisations.

cular, the operational systems of a customer are integrated with those of the vendor. This is much more – in terms of the complexities involved – a problem of integrating production control systems (indeed, up to the level of ERM or enterprise resource management). The electronic communications element, which is typically direct (or by an extranet) rather than by Internet, is for once just a minor part of this. Thus, the benefits depend upon very sophisticated use of stock/production control in the organisations involved. Companies typically have to spend many millions of pounds getting these internal systems working before they can be extended outside the organisation.

Indeed, even though there is now agreement in the US over a (standards) system called EDIfact, this standardisation poses major limitations for most organisations, because

significant investments are needed; perhaps even a restructuring of the whole business. The result is a long start-up
time. Because it is not simple Internet, but relies on dedicated
lines, the communication costs may be expensive, and the
overhead cost of running EDI-type production control
systems should not be neglected. But, all these concern very
sophisticated production control systems, with correspondingly valuable outcomes for those organisations that can
afford them.

EDI on the Internet

Achieving the full benefits of such EDI systems requires very
close integration of the partners' internal systems. On the
other hand, in recent times an attempt has been made to bring
in other vendors who don't possess the same degree of
sophistication – by offering a very simple form of link
through the Internet.

In essence, such systems are little more than extensions of
e-mail, though in a more proscribed format, so that they may
be more easily entered direct into the vendor's computer
systems. Microsoft Outlook is often now used for such
systems. In addition, organisations can use their own extranet
to convey data in their own format. Finally, they can use
outside suppliers who host EDI-type systems for a range of
organisations. Thus Netscape Enterprise offers such a
standardised system for exchanging data.

These may be less sophisticated systems, but the most
important point is that they are much cheaper. The entry cost
can be as little as 1/25th of that of a specialised EDI solution.
As a result, investment can rapidly be covered by the cost
savings, with payback in weeks rather than months and years.
Equally it can be implemented by small companies without
the massive restructuring or cultural upheavals that might
otherwise be needed.

As Internet-based EDI tends to be even more standardised than the more sophisticated systems, it can also reduce switching costs. Traditional EDI systems have tended to be specific to one supply chain. This means that, when switching between suppliers, significant 'switching costs' may be involved. To a large extent this is obviated when a standardised Internet solution is used.

It also means that EDI is only one option in terms of communications between the two organisations. The Internet – and web – connections between the two organisations will expand almost exponentially. This may result in problems of management control, but it does mean that the amount of information available to both sides is dramatically increased.

At the end of the day it is claimed that transaction costs are significantly reduced, but as you have seen – from all the above – that this is probably the least of the benefits of EDI.

Exchanges

Recently, a number of organisations, often the software suppliers involved, have produced what they describe as exchanges, which in theory reflect the idea of commodity exchanges. Thus, they offer to act as intermediaries,

> **KEY CONCEPT**
>
> Business exchanges offer a new way of B2B purchasing.

again using standardised approaches – though since these are vendors of quite sophisticated software, the standardised approaches can be flexible and sophisticated in their own right. Using this sort of approach, members can interchange data for their own production purposes. However, the emphasis so far seems to have been put on obtaining *bids* for supply, in a competitive process. This owes much more to auctions than it does to EDI, and eBay is even now attempting to enter this business. The philosophy here is almost the reverse of EDI. Thus, EDI is based upon considerable co-operation between the partners. This is needed for it to work at the operational level *within* these organisations. The exchanges, conversely, emphasise aggressive competition to lower prices. The core emphasis is on cost *between* the organisations. The exchanges may well suggest that – ideally – members should restrict the list to those organisations which have met the most stringent standards, but at the end of the day *price* is almost all that matters. We should see the sophistication of these operations improving over the years, but there is a long way to go yet.

 ## PAUSE FOR THOUGHT

- If you want to learn more, you should visit the websites of the main vendors, such as SAP.

Business-to-business Internet

The Internet is an ideal way for vendors to obtain feedback from their customers. The easier this process is, the more likely it is to happen. It is an essential part of building business relationships, as well as debugging potential and actual problems. It is also a very easy way of providing help for customers, who can often solve their problems by searching a technical database without waiting for specialised staff from your organisation to assist them. And, for example as used by Dell, it can also offer an ideal vehicle for mass customisation. Customers can specify shop-floor orders for their own products, which are immediately passed to the factory floor for production. In the process customer profiles can also be created, which allow vendors to know much more about their customers' needs.

In this environment the emphasis will probably be on reducing costs, which is what motivated Dell in the first instance. But it may also result in enhanced coverage, and in particular interactive marketing (as described in the section on business-to-consumer markets). Most transactions will probably revolve around the search for information – and the price may be the last element to be asked for, so the whole range of information, from product specifications through to delivery status, may well have to be provided to customers in this way.

E-commerce marketplaces

The emergence of business-to-business communications, and in particular EDI, has often dramatically changed the power relationships between suppliers and purchasers. So, for the sake of completeness, this section will discuss the various marketplaces which have already emerged, or are in the process of emerging. The first key factor which defines how the operation works is whether the process is orientated towards *selling* or *buying*. Thus, in the short term, the main thrust may be from vendors trying to push their products – to make them more easily available to customers. On the other hand, the shift in power has not all been in one direction. Instead, a range of models have emerged.

Supplier-oriented marketplace

The most common model is still that where the supplier controls the marketplace. In essence this looks very much like the normal distribution chain, albeit here it is in the form of an electronic marketplace. It is often a single level marketplace, with disintermediation; in other words, the supplier sells direct to the end user. As suggested above, this is very much the same as the business-to-consumer marketplaces we looked at earlier, especially those relating to the catalogue operations of the clicks and mortar companies. The classic example of this is Dell, which apparently does not distinguish between its sales of PCs to domestic consumers or to industrial conglomerates.

The essence of this is maintaining the relationship over time, through devices such as clubs. But many organisations, even those in the business-to-business marketplace, still look at it as a series of one-off transactions, and accordingly lose much of the benefit that could be gained.

> **KEY CONCEPT**
>
> The e-supplier marketplace is the most common.

It also means that large organisations which place repeated orders face the cost of having to input each of these orders every time. To avoid this, profiles can be produced so that individual purchasers can order standardised packages of goods – and can at the same time get an overall quantity discount. In this way, a staff member who needs supplies of stationery, for example, can open up a window on their PC and order direct from an authorised wholesaler. This means that supplies can be strictly controlled to meet the company's standards (and agreed prices!).

Trust

One thing which is often overlooked is the amount of trust that organisations then place in their authorised vendors. If you are allowing these vendors direct access to your staff at their desks, you must trust them not to abuse the relationship. This means that a great deal of work must be done before such an agreement is made, and afterwards to maintain the relationship.

As a result, a number of new infomediaries are being created which manage this interface for buying organisations. Typically what is being handled is a minor transaction which will not be central to a company's business, but which might severely impact the business if it goes wrong. As a result, these intermediaries will claim that:

1 they are much more effective at searching for the vendors needed, and at providing information about them.
2 they offer quality control, probably not over the product itself but certainly over the information and warranties provided with it.
3 they can be more professional in targeting the company's needs with potential vendors.

Intermediary-oriented marketplaces

These extend the services, hinted at above, to provide a standardised trading platform which offers a credible information source for buyers and sellers – and even goes beyond this to give expert advice for both of them. This category includes the gatekeepers, such as AOL, and ISP providers such as BT. The main activity at present revolves around search engines, finding commercial information for companies. Yahoo! and AltaVista are examples of this, as well as other more sophisticated search engines which search out the best deals among suppliers – typically in terms of prices quoted.

Buyer-oriented marketplaces

The large purchasing organisations can also reverse the model, placing their own business out to tender. But more importantly, following the EDI model, they can create a marketplace which integrates their various suppliers. This can be wider than a single organisation. For example, Ford Motor Company started such a marketplace. A number of other motor manufacturers, most notably General Motors (GM), subsequently joined in. In this way, quantity discounts can even be shared between competitors in the same industry – an unexpected benefit of e-commerce.

 PAUSE FOR THOUGHT

- Which of these marketplaces might be of use in your marketing activities, and how?

Virtual corporations

The idea of a virtual corporation is that it is not buyer-oriented or supplier-oriented, but is an overall integration to produce a virtual business. Here a business may consist of just a handful of people sitting at their desks in a small head office, bringing together suppliers and vendors from around the world to create products and services which the virtual business never sees, but from which it creams off a significant level of profit! These *extraprise* organisations can be seen as a network of people, resources and ideas connected across the Internet.

They offer:

> **KEY CONCEPT**
>
> The virtual business is an interesting concept, but has yet to be widely seen in practice.

- *Excellence* – where each partner is excellent in its specific field, so that the overall offering can be excellent in all respects.
- *Utilisation* – the partners' own facilities and resources can be used to the full, with obvious profit implications.
- *Opportunities* – this synergistic combination can seek out new opportunities which are not available to the individual partners.

But it's not that easy in practice! Problems can still occur, such as:

1   The availability of good information means that the conditions for a commodity market can easily be created – squeezing the partners' profits. In other words, the partners, despite the best intentions, may use the resulting information to squeeze the best deals out of each other – benefiting neither side.
2   Cannibalisation of the value chain may also occur, with partners seeking out the weak elements to incorporate into their own operations.
3   The IT investment demanded across the entire chain may be very expensive if a tightly integrated network is to be created.

Perhaps the trust necessary for this to happen is still in too short supply, for very few successes have yet been recorded in terms of genuinely virtual businesses of this type.

Future developments

CHAPTER 12

Overview

We will finish by looking at some aspects of e-commerce, covering knowledge services in particular, which presently do not feature as large markets, but which may come into their own over the next decade.

The most important of these are consumer-to-business (C2B) and consumer-to-consumer (C2C). At present the former is largely confined to auctions; and indeed to one company, eBay. In future, however, the biggest potential is likely to emerge from the latter, especially from C2C networking. With billions, perhaps trillions, of transactions taking place – through 'affinity networks' – every day between individuals, this has the largest *volume* potential of all. Its *commercial* potential will, though, be subject to the issues we looked at in the section on making money!

Related to the C2C market will be the longer-term developments in the home, especially in the contexts of home-working at one extreme and new lifestyles at the other.

In both cases, the objective of this chapter is to bring these potential developments to your notice, so you will

---

CONTINUED . . . **Overview**

be aware of the potential, and especially the threats, which you may face over the next 10 years.

- Affinity group hosts/portals
- C2C
- E-mail networking
- Electronic conferences
- Lifelong electronic learning
- Computer Aided Instruction (CAI)
- Certification
- Television and books
- Web videos/movies on demand
- Wired houses
- Teleworking
- Self-employment
- Mobile communications
- Wideband

Customer-to-business (C2B)

The only major offering currently widely available in the C2B category is *auctions*. Of these, eBay is dominant, though in Europe QXL now also claims a position, although it is not yet financially secure.

From the point of view of marketing, auctions look very much like their traditional counterparts. eBay claims to have nearly ten million registered users, bidding for some three million items, and each user spends nearly two hours on-site every month, a lot longer than Amazon's equally loyal clientele (but this is probably due to the differing

> **KEY CONCEPT**
>
> The auction house eBay is currently the largest operator in C2B.

natures of the two sites). Partly this is a function of cost – eBay charges 7.5% commission compared with over 25% for some offline auctioneers. The main difference is that, as yet, the traditional business controls imposed by auction houses (for example in vetting buyers and sellers) are largely missing. Thus, the biggest problem, which eBay admits to, is that of fraud – but its only answer to this, with which it seems quite happy, is caveat emptor! From a business point of view the good thing is, as eBay claims, once you build the software the whole thing runs itself. The sellers and buyers do all the work – the home site just creams off the 7.5% commission.

It is important to note, however, that eBay now has wider ambitions – even aiming to add on a 'business exchange'! In the C2B sector it has a customer base which it might be able to leverage to gain the type of customer-based business from which Letsbuyit.com failed to make money. At present the best way to learn about C2B is to visit the eBay website.

Consumer-to-consumer or customer-to-customer

In many respects, this is an untapped market – at least in commercial terms. As we will see later, there may be considerable potential but the means of unlocking this potential has not yet been exploited.

In particular, it is not yet clear how this marketplace might develop, though it is obvious that its ultimate potential could be very large indeed. One of the things that will be needed, though, is a range of intermediaries who will host the various activities.

> **KEY CONCEPT**
>
> In the longer term C2C will be the largest market.

Affinity group hosts and portals

It is true that many of the activities will be bilateral, or even multilateral, and organised by the individuals involved. The new eBay approach does not address this, though the AOL user groups might develop into something like this. But eventually it seems likely that there will be specialist organisations who will act as intermediaries in these types of transactions. Thus, they will host the communications and the exploitation of potential. They will then manage the exchange of information, for a price (both to be paid to the originator of the information, and to the intermediaries for their services). Finally, they will arrange for payments to take place in order for the information and any physical items, or services, to be bought.

Having said all that, there is currently – apart from the portals who would claim to be able to do anything you want – nothing designed to offer this sort of service. But watch this space!

> **KEY CONCEPT**
>
> Portals are best placed to exploit C2C.

E-mail

Currently, e-mail – memos in organisations and correspondence between individuals in the home sector – probably represents the major use of C2C. Certainly in terms of numbers of users, if not volume of transactions, such person-to-person communication has the greatest market penetration of all. Written communication has long been the backbone of business, and even of private communication. E-mail can be seen as the latest extension of this. As such, it is the most

> **KEY CONCEPT**
>
> C2C e-mail provides the main volume of traffic over the Internet, but is not yet widely used as part of e-commerce.

important new form of human communication to emerge since the telephone, yet remarkably little attention has been paid to its new rules.

However, we are ill-prepared for e-mail. Our education system still emphasises the teaching of the three Rs, where in real life our pupils now have to go far beyond this to use the much more sophisticated technologies which the Internet and other electronic communications make available. It is true that the basis is still the written word, at the moment printed or typed and soon verbal (with audio input starting to escalate), but a much wider range of communications routes are also now available.

In this, almost trivial, context it is worth putting some effort into designing your e-mail formats – in a similar way to how you design your business letterheads. Very few of us bother to do this, but you can very easily incorporate some useful information in such a way, especially in your sign-off lines. These should contain your website address, where your recipients can find out more about you. But even so, and perhaps just as important, it should also contain your telephone number (and preferably also your address). So many communications over the Internet fail for one reason or another and such traditional backup relieves frustrations on the part of people who can't get in touch with you when this happens. Such details may cumulatively create more impact than your advertising in the mass media! Perhaps as important, the recipients of your e-mails will judge you by their content.

On the subject of receiving e-mails from customers, you might also like to consider some techniques which can improve service. One, for e-mails directed at specific addresses on your

> **KEY CONCEPT**
>
> E-mail techniques are relatively undeveloped.

site, may be to use an 'auto-responder', which automatically sends out a detailed reply, for example enlarging on the information provided on the main website. This saves effort on your part and, more importantly, speeds up your response to the customer. In any case, you should always send (again via an auto-responder) an immediate confirmation that you have received the e-mail and an indication that you are dealing with it. This should also contain the URL of the website which details FAQs (the answers to Frequently Asked Questions), so that the customer can see if their problem has already been solved before you reply formally.

 ## PAUSE FOR THOUGHT

■ The practical exercise you can now undertake is to review your own e-mail options – and design the most effective sign-off lines. You can also look at using an auto-responder to provide immediate acknowledgement of messages received.

Electronic conferences and bulletin boards

A particular form of e-mail is an electronic computer conference, or bulletin board – sometimes also referred to as a message board, or discussion forum. These are addresses on which you can leave messages for other people to come and look at; hence the concept of messages being pinned on to a bulletin board. These conferences have become much more sophisticated over recent years. They're very effective at sharing communications, especially because the sender of the message only has to send it to one site for it to be made available to a large number of people.

So far this chapter has discussed what can be described as formal conferencing, although one aspect of electronic conferencing, which has a life of its own, is the *chat room* –

often, unlike most other Internet activities, carried out in real time. There is no formal agenda, as people just get together to chat – much as they might at a cocktail party – and gregarious people seem to like them, even if the content of many chat rooms is overtly sexual.

> **KEY CONCEPT**
>
> Electronic conferences offer a powerful new means of communication, somewhere between face-to-face and mass media.

Technology is becoming ever more sophisticated, extending to real-time audio communication (with whiteboards, which means that while talking you can also draw diagrams which are transmitted across the conference) and videoconferencing. At the moment the latter is fairly crude, limited by communications line speeds, but – as the DSL and cable modem systems become more widespread – use will improve dramatically. It is argued that, within ten years or so, very large screens, which occupy almost a whole wall, will be available. These could be made of plasma or liquid crystal, or simply projected screens, but the point about them is that – especially if they employ three-dimensional techniques – it will look as if the person you're talking to is sharing a room with you. When this happens, videoconferencing may escalate rapidly. It will add a new dimension to social contact. You will be able to regularly 'meet' all your friends and family – even if they are on the other side of the world!

Accordingly, a growing aspect of such communications is the more sophisticated forms of audio- and visual-tele-conferencing, which allow meetings to be personally 'attended' by participants from anywhere in the world. This technology is now in use by a number of organisations for internal communications and it has now been reduced in price to such an extent that the long-promised video-phone may soon become viable even for domestic use. Its (synchronous) use over the Internet, however, is not compatible with the (asynchronous) packet-switching approach used by the

Internet. Accordingly, it will require careful design, a suitable software package (such as CU-SeeMe, which is the most widely used at present) and high bandwidth before it becomes more generally viable. Even now, however, I do most of my radio interviews down an ISDN line without ever visiting the studio. I suspect that quite soon I will do the same for my television work!

The inevitable problem for person-to-person communication is, as it was with the telephone when it was first launched, that you need the person at the other end of the line also to have a video phone. In fact for *any* type of real-time communication you also need the person on the other end of the line to be there, even if it's just to tap messages into a keyboard! One of the main advantages, perhaps, of ordinary e-mails – which we often forget about – is that they are asynchronous and you can leave them for recipients to pick them up at their convenience. You never get an engaged signal or have to rely on an answering machine.

 PAUSE FOR THOUGHT

■ Using your existing marketing knowledge, and the e⁺marketing knowledge you have now acquired, review how effectively the various conferences you administer operate. How may they be improved?

New consumer-to-consumer (C2C) developments

This is a speculative area, so the only advice I will give here is to keep your eyes and ears open. As yet there has been very little happening, but the potential is such that, maybe very soon, developments *will* occur. If you are to get on the bandwagon when these do occur you will have to recognise the signs that will precede such developments. Unfortunately, I can't even help you by telling you what those symptoms may be. This is the ultimate example where environmental scanning is essential!

Life long learning (LLL)

I have already suggested that meeting the needs of the new lifestyles may be one of the big new markets on the Internet. Another one, in the short- to medium-term, which is almost guaranteed, is that of education.

Once more, however, you have to beware the hype. You will find that many educational providers, both public and private but especially the institutions that like to think they're at the leading edge of technology,

> **KEY CONCEPT**
>
> LLL will be the largest e-commerce market in the medium term.

will offer you computer- or Internet-delivered courses. The problem here is the technology of *distance learning*, something we at the Open University are well aware of – it is our livelihood. As yet we have not found a cost-effective means of making the best use of the interactive capabilities of computer education over the Internet. Our current material can be equally well delivered by the postman, and such printed material is much cheaper to support. Even so, as an indication of the investment levels needed, it still costs the best part of one million pounds to run each major course. We do use electronic communications for some parts of our business, including general communications and submissions of the student exercises; in particular, we make considerable use of electronic conferences to bring students together. Distance learning students often feel isolated, and giving them an electronic conference – so they can talk with fellow students – helps to ameliorate this. Paradoxically, though, the greatest advantage is that such computer conferences typically stimulate them to set up a local self-help group, where they can meet other students face-to-face. One of the great counter-intuitive facts about electronic communication between individuals is that it works best if the individuals can – from time to time – meet rather than, as normally recommended, when they are so remote that they never meet!

Computer-aided instruction (CAI)

The problem here is that the main providers have not yet managed to productively incorporate computer-based teaching (CBT) or, as it is often now called, computer-aided instruction (CAI) into their offerings. Thus, even in Open University material, what you typically get is large chunks of text which could be in any textbook. Between these slabs of text we insert activities, which the students complete, to consolidate what they have just learned.

We now increasingly use PC-based systems to allow students to test themselves, using multiple-choice questions. We then provide a degree of feedback, explaining whether they

> **KEY CONCEPT**
>
> Effective CAI is not yet generally available.

are right or wrong and, if wrong, what the correct answer was. Truly effective computer-aided instruction comes, though, when this feedback is used to *manage* the progress of the student. Thus, in theory at least, depending upon how well they have learned the lesson you may allow them to skip the next unit – because they already understand enough. Perhaps more likely, they may have learned it so badly that you have to return them to the beginning of the previous section. This is all about managing the student's *individual progress*.

Some software for doing this is available, in crude form, but it needs to be significantly enhanced. More importantly, you have to put much more effort into developing the material it uses, typically providing at least three times as much information (where you have to cater for all the alternative answers and in particular the interactions with the management system). This is where most systems currently are held up. CAI is not a cost-free solution!

Our own forecasts suggested that the best people to get round this problem – and produce the most popular education programmes using technology very similar to that now available in the games market – would either be the IT multinationals (especially Microsoft) or the Hollywood studios. The logistics of it are very similar to those of making a film – and in fact the most expensive part is making the moving pictures which illustrate the programme. To our surprise, this does not yet appear to have happened.

Certification

In general, the first problem – and possibly the most insuperable in the shorter tem – for the individual and for the many small providers, will be the vast choice available. It will be difficult to trawl through the literally hundreds of thousands of offerings to find one which matches your individual needs – even with the new artificial intelligence agents – let alone find guaranteed quality. In the case of education it is not just your money you may waste but your time, and that is often much more valuable. So we're likely to see the emergence of various initiatives to host certification authorities. In the UK the government's eUniversity goes some way towards that, though it is taking much longer to set up than most people allowed for.

PAUSE FOR THOUGHT

- A personally useful exercise would be to trawl the Internet to see which providers of distance learning in general, and of electronically delivered material in particular, might have offerings which would be of interest to you. Compare them: not in terms of how pretty their websites are, but how effectively they deliver the education they offer.
- A good starting point is with the UK's Open University, which is a world-leader in distance learning. You can find it at www.open.ac.uk.

Television and books

The ubiquitous PC may not remain unchallenged for ever. Digitisation of television, which is growing rapidly and will be widespread within the next decade, will also make significant steps in terms of education – not least because of the hundreds of TV channels which may be available. Some of these, such as Discovery, already verge on being education deliverers – and many more may enter this market. For example, the BBC's Learning Zone is directed towards this. Indeed, it is arguable that television is already the main source of education amongst the population. People tend to think of it just as 'the box' sitting in the corner providing light entertainment, but you don't notice just how much information it provides you with – even if you only follow soap operas. The most ignorant person today probably knows more about the world as a whole than the best-educated person in Victorian times.

Until quite recently, I thought that electronic books would not have a great impact. But I have had a rethink on this, since we're getting close to the time when devices the size of books, with screens that look very much like books and in many respects – apart from that lovely smell of new printing ink – will work just as well as printed books. When this happens, electronic books

<table>
<tr><td>KEY CONCEPT

Digital television, and eventually electronic books, will significantly increase in importance, not least in terms of LLL.</td></tr>
</table>

will be just as portable as conventional books. But then we will also start to see the benefit of hyperlinking to other knowledge bases. These will then become available, when you want them, from within that book (whther this is a novel or a reference book).

Computing at home

To give an indication of longer-term developments, this section will explore something which is not currently in the mainstream for most managers or their organisations – the development of personalised computing in the home. In recent years this has been somewhat confused by the battle between the Internet and the superhighway. The concept of the Internet, at least in the business environment, was well understood as an answer to one-to-one personal communi-cation. The superhighway, on the other hand, was picked up by the television channels, especially in the US. To put it at its crudest level, they saw it in terms they recognised – as 1000-channel TV. This is at the opposite end of the spectrum to the one-to-one nature of the Internet. The split is also at the heart of AOL Time-Warner. AOL represents Internet anarchy and Time-Warner is the 1000-channel superhighway. It will be interesting to see how, or even if, the resulting conglomerate prospers!

This split has somewhat bedevilled the home superhigh-way. But now the technology behind the two, though not the philosophy of the two, has converged. The newest games stations have very sophisticated Internet capabilities built into them – and increasingly digital televisions have equally sophisticated communications facilities. So far they are mainly used as a means of placing orders against a home shopping channel, but the technology is there for future development.

Ultimately, though, the home communications element will grow. The Internet is potentially, for all of us, a way of creating the global village that Marshall McLuhan dreamed of in the 1960s. It really is as easy, and as cheap, to talk through the Internet to someone on the other side of the world as it is to do the same to someone on the next desk. I run one computer conference with over 600 members who come from the depths of Siberia and Alaska, as well as most of the developing nations. The interesting part is that when I am conversing with them I really don't know whether they're in a mud hut or a penthouse on Park Avenue in New York.

Video

As I have said, much of the technology has emerged already. You can obtain television pictures, not least from web cameras, and this even extends to video-conferencing on your own desktop PC. As yet, the pictures from these web-cams are quite crude but soon, when high-speed communication is available through all the stages of the communications link right to the office or the home, they will be as good as any you now see on the entertainment channels.

Equally, the Internet communications facilities on digital televisions are already as comprehensive and sophisticated as those on your PC. The difference, then, is in the philosophy behind the promotional strategies for each. Thus the Internet for the

KEY CONCEPT

Video communications will soon become widespread, and will offer an important new mode of communication.

office is very much driven by the user, and is focused on one-to-one communications capabilities. The digital television, however, is seen as a means of access to the entertainment channels. You will no doubt see the two converge, but at the moment there is a distinct difference between them.

 ## PAUSE FOR THOUGHT

- What impact will such video contact have on your work and your private life?

Wired house, wired individual

But, as the technology converges, the computers themselves will become *invisible*. They will disappear into the fabric of the house. This will be particularly true where there is wireless technology, such as Bluetooth, enabling the whole house to be covered by just one server. Every device will then contain a (Bluetooth) chip so it can communicate with the server. This means that all the services within the home may then be easily controlled. It also means that you can be in communication with the rest of the world wherever you are in the house – and even outside it, as you move through other Bluetooth domains.

One result of this will be that the preoccupation with the PC, and its related technology, will disappear. It will no longer even be seen. To illustrate this, I like to use the analogy of the

> **KEY CONCEPT**
>
> ICT developments will have a major impact on the design of the home.

aristocracy in the older days. They had many servants, as we now have many computers, but they never noticed them.

Servants were there to serve you when you needed them. In future, computers will replace servants.

 PAUSE FOR THOUGHT

- What implications does this have in terms of the changes you will need to make to your own house?

Working in Nepal!

The new communications capabilities will enable us to change our way of life. Some of us may decide to decamp to the hills of Nepal. It will be just as easy to locate your office there as it will in the middle of London. Today, some of my colleagues spend the summer in Tuscany, writing their books in that very pleasant environment. On the other hand the seductive concept of the 'electronic cottage' – with you working at your desk looking out into a beautiful forest glade – is unlikely to be a reality for most people. The view from your window will still be that of suburbia! But, some of us may instead choose to *visit* the hills of Nepal electronically – while sitting comfortably at home in suburbia – saving ourselves the hassle of a long flight to an exotic destination.

Teleworking

The ultimate outcome of these dramatic changes in communications may well be that we will spend more time working at home. I already spend most of my time working at home, although I live only half a mile away from the Open University where I also have an office. It's a pleasant life. But there are still problems. Paradoxically, IT technology is not the main problem. These days, or very soon, most of us in the developed world will have a fibre-optic link past our front door. Even in the Third World it is now possible for relatively simple equipment to send signals via satellite. The real problem is the *physical* structure of our housing. At home, I am very fortunate in having many more office facilities than other teleworkers: including, in particular, an office which is 20 feet by 20 feet.

Realistically, for one person to work at home, you will need a room that is at least the size of a double bedroom. Unfortunately the current norm for most workers is the three-bedroom house, so the problem is really how to find the equivalent of

> **KEY CONCEPT**
>
> The greatest limitation on tele-working – which will rapidly grow in importance – will be the physical space needed for a viable home office.

that double bedroom. The spare bedroom, even in four-bedroom houses, really won't do. What is needed is the equivalent of the second bedroom in a *five*-bedroom house! As you will appreciate, the difference in capital value of a five-bedroom house versus a three-bedroom one, is possibly an order of magnitude. Few people can afford to make this upgrade, and in any case it probably takes, in the UK at least, something like a century for the housing stock to turn over. So, even if, supported by our employers and government, we wanted to work at home it would take a number of decades before this was achievable. Incidentally, the UK government may well *want* us to do this, since cutting down on our travel time to work would substantially reduce the increasingly heavy load on the transport infrastructure.

 PAUSE FOR THOUGHT

- How would this change your life?
- How would you need to change your home?

Cost savings?

The picture is a lot less clear about the supposed cost savings to be attributed to teleworking. It is generally true that the cost of space in the home is much less than that in a city centre, but on the other side of the equation there are other support costs. As we have seen, the romantic idea that you can work on the kitchen table with the children playing around you just isn't true. Equally you will, as soon as you start to work at home for a significant period, realise just how much support is available to you in the office – you may even have to learn how to make your own coffee at home!

There is also a social price to play, in that working from home can feel very isolated, and most teleworkers will also still need a desk in a central office. This means that it is much more realistic to expect, even if all the other problems are sorted out and space made available in the home, people to work at home three days out of five, and the other two to be spent in the office socialising and carrying out work that cannot be done at home.

> **KEY CONCEPT**
>
> The main drivers towards teleworking will initially be social rather than financial.

In terms of physical space considerations, incidentally, the best guess at this stage is that the new boom industry will be that of converting double garages, or even conservatories, into home offices, so the big growth areas of the construction industry in recent history will have to go into reverse. On the other hand, it is reasonable to assume that, even if only part of the time is spent working at home, the family will then only need one car. As a result, there may be enough space in the double garage to slot in a new (factory-built) pod – the new home office.

Part-time, self-employed work

This is a rather different phenomenon which is linked to teleworking. The result may be that – even without teleworking – we will have a portfolio of jobs. Increasingly the barriers between companies in the outside world are dissolving. This development started with the move to re-engineering in the 1990s. That was largely a cynical move, by large corporations, to shift costs out of the company itself. Its prime aim was to reduce costs – not least because there was a pool of unemployed people willing to beat down prices. The boot is now on the other foot.

We're moving to a time of significant skills shortage. This means that employers will become increasingly desperate to recruit personnel. The problem is that those displaced personnel are now very happy to work as contract workers, or part-time employees. They see many advantages, not least the fact that, due to the skills shortage, they can set their own rates. This means that many individuals will start to sell their skills to different employers at the same time, so they may have a port-folio of jobs spread across a number of companies. This may, over time, become quite a stable portfolio. They may still choose to work mainly for one employer, but even this may be as a freelance. The rest of their time may well be spent working for a range of employers – on one day a month contracts, or even on a contingency basis. The most interesting aspect of this, however, is that the group most likely to adopt this way of life will be the *older* workers – those aged 50 years or over. They have the financial reserves which make it possible, and increasingly subscribe to the idea that work should be some-thing you enjoy, or at least find fulfilling! Although teleworking is not essential for this to happen, it will of course significantly enhance the process, and accelerate its introduction.

Other electronic media

Although this book is largely about management concerns, it still worthwhile to record some of the other uses the Internet will be put to in the home.

Movies on demand

As I said earlier, one of the aspects that Hollywood expected to emerge was movies on demand, or at least 1000-channel TV. No doubt something like this will eventually emerge, although the form it is currently taking is more like several hundred copies each of a few blockbusters, rather than 1000 different films. This is so that you can find one that will start within the next five minutes or so, for an impatient audience, rather than adding to your choice.

Also as a result of the increasing number of channels, which was already happening as a result of the penetration of cable channels in the US, there are more and more specialist channels. Some of these

> **KEY CONCEPT**
>
> Movies-on-demand will be less important than Hollywood expected.

have made a significant contribution to knowledge. Discovery Channel, for instance, is one that competes on its own terms with public service broadcasting.

Again, not necessarily as a result of the Internet but more a result of the proliferation of channels in general, the news services may well benefit, with news from around the world being broadcast in real-time.

Mobile telecommunications

There has been a lot of hype about mobile telecommunications. This, I suspect, derives from the very rapid growth of mobile telephones. Mobile phones make a lot of sense – though that probably isn't why people buy them! Having just one fixed telephone in your house means that you can only be contacted at home. Being able to carry a telephone with you everywhere is a major boon.

This is not to say that Internet facilities will proliferate on such 3G phones in the same way. The court is still out on this, and companies that paid such high prices in auctions for the new wavelengths may find it difficult to recoup these costs! There is only a limited amount of information that can fit on the small screen of any phone. On the other hand, some form of mobile book or digital assistant, which has a larger screen and audio input, may be a very different proposition. So look for the expansion of mobile books – publishers especially should take note of this.

> **KEY CONCEPT**
>
> Communications will be increasingly mobile, but not through mobile phones as such – and will not repay the massive investments made in the bandwidth auctions.

High-speed access

Many of the most dramatic uses of the Internet, especially those revolving around video communication, which will take off when the facilities are available, will depend upon the presence of a high-speed communications line. These are becoming available on many, if not most, telephone exchanges. The missing link is between those exchanges and the home; the so-called 'local loop'. DSL or ADSL are protocols which enable existing telephone lines to transmit information at speeds of up to 2 megabits per second (Mbps).

This is sufficient to get fairly crude television pictures down the line, and these can be easily upgraded later by fibre optics to produce the high-quality television pictures which will soon be required. Access can also be through cable modems. In this case your cable supplier simply allows you to tap into their coaxial network. This allows even faster transmissions speeds. Unfortunately these must be shared

> **KEY CONCEPT**
>
> High-speed access will soon be widely available, at a low price, and will drive the widespread introduction of video applications.

with the other users on your spur, which means that transmission speeds may be limited by a growing number of users. The more users there are, the slower will be the speed of the individual line. Again, though, replacing coaxial cable with fibre optics will remove this limitation.

So, by whatever means, the line into the office – and in particular the line into the home – can, and soon will, be upgraded to handle anything we might want in the foreseeable future.

Overall, the emphasis will be on *convergence* and *invisibility*. In other words, these services will start to disappear into the fabric of our homes and of our lives. We will not worry about the technology, or how it gets to us. Televisions were seen as miraculous less than a century ago, yet now our main technical problem is how to handle the timer on our video recorder. We take the technology that delivers moving pictures from the moon to our living room for granted. The Internet, and e-commerce, will soon fall into the same category.

 PAUSE FOR THOUGHT

- Once again, think a while. How will these changes affect your working life and your private life?

Conclusion

CHAPTER 13

It may seem as if my suggestion at the beginning of the book, that e-commerce follows most of the marketing rules that have been established in conventional markets, may have been overtaken by all the differences listed in the 60,000 or so words you have read since! The truth is somewhere between the two extremes.

The first statement I must reiterate is that e-commerce marketing builds on what you have learned for conventional markets. Your starting point,

> **KEY CONCEPT**
>
> E-commerce marketing builds upon existing marketing skills.

before you consider anything else, still must be traditional marketing theory and technique! The second statement, and the justification for the 'e⁺marketing' concept introduced in Chapter 1, is that the major part of e-commerce concerns organisations moving into this sector from more traditional ones – where they will already be deploying a rich mix of marketing activities.

On the other hand, there are some significant differences, which you ignore at your peril. The main difference has little to do with the ICT

> **KEY CONCEPT**
>
> In practice, CRM is a main driver.

technology, which is at best seen as an enabler. It is, instead, the recent recognition of the importance of customer relationship management (CRM). The value of e-commerce, in this context, is that for the first time it allows the possibility of genuine one-to-one marketing, even in mass markets. So, the main lessons to be learned are those of (one-to-one) CRM, such as lifestyle and permission marketing.

But, in addition to relationships with individual customers, we will also have to deal with the electronic communities to which they belong – and with which they communicate in ever more complex networks. Maintaining relations with all of these will demand a rich new mix of skills including in database management.

In terms of the specific elements of the marketing mix, the most important thing to remember is that much of what is described as e-commerce is in fact just one element of the overall marketing mix. The balance of *all* the elements in the mix is what matters!

Within the mix, however, the segmentation and positioning aspects are just as important – though here they may relate to segments of one individual. The marketing research associated with this may be much less effective, in terms of group averages, since the sampling frameworks are not yet available. But this does not matter where information is available, instead, about the individual. Even so, branding may be even more important, where so much of the offering is otherwise intangible. Pricing should be on a premium basis, where the matching of individual requirements is central to activities and there is little opportunity to create any economies of scale, but in reality commodity pricing still rules.

To service all these new markets, a range of new providers is emerging, ranging from syndicators to ASPs to portals, but these will all have to make their services easy to use in terms of ease of navigation backed up by guaranteed content.

The most obvious lessons are to be learned in the e-retail sector, and especially from direct marketing and catalogue selling. The rule of thumb lessons previously learned in this sector, from the techniques of direct mail to the management of clubs, are those that are most applicable to the new field of e-commerce – even though they have previously been overlooked by marketing academics.

The biggest problem for participating organisations in all e-commerce sectors, is still how to make money out of it. Advertising does not seem to be the way, for most organisations. Acting as (paid)

> **KEY CONCEPT**
>
> The biggest challenge is how to make money from e-commerce.

intermediaries in C2C is some way off. So, for the time being, the best suggestion seems to be to earn commissions or royalties for your services – but in a market where so much is still free this will be no easy matter!

Much of business-to-business (B2B) will follow the same pattern as B2C, for most organisations. For a few of the larger organisations, EDI will allow significant productivity gains – but the driver here will still be operations management rather than e-commerce.

Ultimately, the customer-to-customer (C2C) sector will be the most valuable, with affinity groups lying at the heart of marketing activities, but this sector still has a long way to go. In the medium term,

> **KEY CONCEPT**
>
> C2C will ultimately hold the greatest potential.

selling lifestyles (or managing them) will be important but, before that, distance education will probably become the largest industry in this sector.

Finally, the greatest impacts will come when the radical changes in society, such as teleworking, filter through. Then our lives will all become quite different. But that will not take place for a few decades yet.

Coventry University

BIBLIOGRAPHY

Bayne, Kim M (2000) *Internet Marketing Plan: the Complete Guide to Instant Web Presence, 2nd ed*, John Wiley & Sons Inc, New York.

Cannon, Jeff (2000) *Make your Website Work for you: How to Convert your Online Content into Profits*, CommerceNet Press, McGraw Hill, New York.

Chaffey, Dave (2000) *Internet Marketing: Strategy, Implementation and Practice*, Financial Times Prentice Hall, Harlow.

Clegg, Brian (2000) *Invisible Customer: Strategies for Successful Customer Service Down the Wire*, Kogan Page, London.

Collin, Simon (2000) *E-marketing*, John Wiley & Sons Ltd, Chichester.

Gabay, J Jonathan (2000) *Successful Cybermarketing in a Week*, Hodder and Stoughton, London.

Gad, Thomas (2001) *4D Branding: Cracking the Corporate Code of the Network Economy*, Financial Times Prentice Hall, London.

Heller, Robert and Spenley, Paul (2000) *Riding the Revolution: How Businesses can and must Transform themselves to Win the E-Wars*, HarperCollins, London.

Kimball, Ralph and Merz, Richard (2000) *Data Webhouse Toolkit: Building the Web Enabled Data Warehouse*, John Wiley & Sons Inc, New York.

Kotabe, Masaaki and Helsen, Kristiaan (2001) *Global Marketing Management, 2nd ed*, John Wiley & Sons Inc, New York.

Lindstrom, Martin and Andersen, Tim Frank (2000) *Brand Building on the Internet*, Kogan Page, London.

Newall, Frederick (2000) *Loyalty.com: Customer Relationship Management in the New Era of Internet Marketing*, McGraw Hill, New York.

O'Malley, Lisa, Patterson, Maurice and Evans, Martin (1999) *Exploring Direct Marketing*, International Thomson Business Press, London.

Seybold, Patricia B (1998) *Customers.com: How to Create a Profitable Business Strategy for the Internet and Beyond*, London Century Business.

Walters, Rob (1997) *CTI in Action,* John Wiley & Sons Ltd, Chichester.

INDEX